Saveur Cooks Authentic Italian

SAVEUR
COOKS

AUTHENTIC
ITALIAN

Savoring the Recipes and Traditions of the World's Favorite Cuisine

by the editors of Saveur *magazine*

CHRONICLE BOOKS

SAN FRANCISCO

First Chronicle Books LLC paperback edition,
published in 2008

ISBN 978-0-8118-6574-6
The Library of Congress has cataloged the previous
edition as follows:

Saveur cooks authentic Italian : savoring the recipes
and traditions of the world's favorite cuisine / by the
editors of Saveur magazine.
             p. cm.
         Includes index
         ISBN 0-8118-3267-8
         1. Cookery, Italian. I. Saveur.

    TX723 .S342 2001
    641.5945—dc21

    2001028037

Printed in China.

10 9 8 7 6 5 4 3 2 1

Chronicle Books LLC
680 Second Street
San Francisco, California 94107

www.chroniclebooks.com

Acknowledgments

IT WAS INEVITABLE that we produce *Saveur Cooks Authentic Italian*. While our heads are sometimes turned by a whiff of Thai or our imaginations caught by some French dish or other, when we come home at night, almost every night, Italian is what we make for dinner. *Saveur Cooks Authentic Italian* is the third book by the editors of SAVEUR magazine. Our first, *Saveur Cooks Authentic American*, published in 1998, won the James Beard Foundation's Award for Best American Cookbook. It was followed, in 1999, by *Saveur Cooks Authentic French*. As with those books, a core group of editors produced this one: Colman Andrews, Editor, whose singular writing style and deep knowledge of all things Italian inform every page; Executive Editor Christopher Hirsheimer, who not only researched and produced many of the stories and their recipes but photographed them as well; our devoted Managing Editor, Ann McCarthy, who took our boisterous crew in hand and craftily coerced them into meeting deadlines (there *was* the magazine to get out); our bilingual Project Editor, Silvana Nardone, who guided the research. The book was shaped by the superb editorial instincts of its designer, Toby Fox, once SAVEUR's Associate Art Director, and by Creative Director Michael Grossman, who helped set the series' style. We appreciate Photography Editor Maya Kaimal and Assistant Editor Amy Lundeen; the eagle eyes of our Copy Chief, Judith Sonntag, and John Guida; and our tenacious research team: Francesca Granata; Shoshana Goldberg, Anna Painter, Marianne Recher, and Megan Wetherall. The proficient Chloe Osborne tested our recipes, aided by our test kitchen's own Melissa Hamilton and Julia Lee. Jenny Chung, Julie Pryma, and Eric Janes ensured the rich production qualities our publications are known for.

We are deeply grateful to our touchstones in all things Italian, Marcella and Victor Hazan, Lidia Bastianich, and Darrell Corti—generous authorities who were always available to help us sort out tetchy problems. To make this book, we've poked around some of the most enticing kitchens in Italy: traveling to a tiny village in the Ligurian *entroterra* to witness the making of the definitive torta and to the port of Palermo in Sicily in search of ice cream; learning lasagne in the town where it was born—Bologna—and capturing the recipes we've loved for decades from the storied restaurants of Rome. We have drawn on the work of some of the great photographers and writers who regularly appear in our magazine; photography credits appear on page 310. The writers are Eugenia Bone, Lori Zimring De Mori, David Downie, David Karp, Peggy Knickerbocker, Thomas McNamee, Marlene Parrish, Robert Ragaini, Vincent Schiavelli, William Sertl, and our own Deputy Editor, Margo True. We thank Cullen Stanley, our agent at Janklow & Nesbit, for leading us through another book. At Chronicle Books, we thank our editor, Bill LeBlond—three's a charm, Bill—and the Chronicle team, Benjamin Shaykin, Tera Killip, Jan Hughes, and Amy Treadwell. Thanks, too, to Terry Snow, owner of World Publications; to Publisher Gregg Hano; and to all the rest of our beloved colleagues at SAVEUR magazine. —DOROTHY KALINS, *Editor-in-Chief*, SAVEUR

Table of Contents

INTRODUCTION

HERE WE ARE in Italy at last—waking

up on the overnight train as it clatters into

Domodossola, at the foot of the Simplon

Pass; descending on the over-night from

JFK through smoky mist over fields of

A fishermen's market in Bari, on the Adriatic coast, left, probably in the 1950s. Customers eat raw shellfish at wooden tables in the background.

yellowed grain into Malpensa, gateway to gray Milan; stretching on the deck of the blunt-faced ferry from Barcelona, watching as the tiered, crowded majesty of Genoa comes slowly into focus in the soft northern Mediterranean light…. However and whenever we arrive in Italy, the first thing we want to do—before we check in to our hotel or rent our car; sometimes even before we step outside the train station or terminal or airport—is eat. Maybe it's just a cornetto, the lightly glazed Italian croissant, and a jolt of coffee—pure coffee, distilled down into a thick black draft, related to our usual morning brew as fine cognac is to flabby wine; maybe it's a glass of trebbiano or sangiovese and an Italian sandwich—real salami, salty and moist, on pizza-dough bread, or a fluffy little hard-shelled roll filled with sliced fontina; maybe it's a plate of pasta, a tangle of noodles with a few ounces of sauce, toothsome, steaming, full of simple flavor. It's the way we reconnect with Italy, the way we assure ourselves that we're really there.

Of course, we don't get these cravings only in the place itself. We walk around that way; we have Italian food on our minds, often, everywhere, right now. It's what we think

Workers in the aging room at a parmigiano-reggiano factory in Parma in the 1950s, left.

PARMIGIANO-REGGIANO

I t is the ultimate Italian cheese, used throughout the peninsula; it is essential to a host of classic dishes, from Liguria's pesto to Campania's parmigiana di melanzane; it is also prized as the finest of Italy's table cheeses, eaten in firm, salty little chunks the color of ancient ivory. There are at least 200 distinct varieties of formaggio in Italy, 30 of them bearing the European Community's D.O.P., or Protected Designation of Origin, but parmigiano-reggiano is Il Re, the king. Named for the cities of Parma and Reggio nell'Emilia, historic centers of its production, it is made only in a precisely defined zone covering portions of five north-central Italian provinces, four in Emilia-Romagna and one in neighboring Lombardy. Similar cheeses are made

elsewhere in northern Italy under the generic name *grana*, for their granular texture; the best of these is grana padano. (American "parmesan" has nothing to do with any of these and is best left on the shelf.) Parmigiano-reggiano, or just plain parmigiano, is a cow's-milk cheese, originally made mostly from the milk of a medieval breed called *razza reggiana* (or *vacca rossa*—red cow), although these have been replaced in recent years by other breeds. At its best, parmigiano has a nutty, earthy flavor, pronounced but not overbearing, and a grain that feels a bit like cornmeal in the mouth. Young (it must be aged for at least a year before sale), it melts into sauces; older, it is best eaten alone, in golden shards. Even the rind of parmigiano is used—put into soups and sauces to add flavor.

WINE & VINEGAR

The Greeks called the Italian peninsula *Oenotria*, the land of cultivated vines—and they should have known, since they introduced grape-growing and wine making there. Today, wine is made in every one of Italy's 20 regions, and the country is the world's leading wine producer. The overwhelming majority of Italian wine is literally everyday stuff, drunk with no ceremony. But something approaching 20 percent of it is now classified with a denomination of origin, a DOC or DOCG, theoretically guaranteeing a certain standard of quality (although some of Italy's finest wines remain unclassified, usually because they use nontraditional grape varieties). The complex barolos and barbarescos of Piedmont; the sensuous, earthy chiantis and brunellos of Tuscany; the fragrant, minerally

whites of Friuli and the Veneto; the ripe, ebullient reds of Campania; the sun-drenched sweet wines of Sicily—these are only a few of Italy's wine treasures. Wherever there is wine, of course, there is also vinegar—which is not, as it's sometimes called, wine gone bad but rather wine taken in a different direction, acetified, honed to sharpness. The Italians favor vinegar as a medium of preservation, especially for cooked vegetables and fish (as in the classic Venetian sarde in saor; see page 182), and use it regularly for dressing salads. Balsamic vinegar? A footnote; a delicious curiosity. Until recently, it was rarely seen outside Emilia-Romagna and was used there as a precious condiment (drizzled on strawberries or parmigiano, for instance), never wasted on lettuce or in cooking.

about when our stomach starts to growl. It's what's for dinner—if we're lucky. Chinese food tempts us with its humor and imagination; we love French food for its intelligent complexity and its poetic soul; the cooking of America is nearest to our heart because it is our mother's milk, our daily bread, the roots that nourish us. But the food of Italy appeals to us, seduces us, makes itself indispensable to us, by its sheer sensory confidence—by simply being there, accessible, satisfying, always.

Time and again, surveys show that we Americans eat Italian more than any other "foreign" food; if you count pizza, in its take-out-window, speedy-delivery incarnations, the competition isn't even close. What is it about Italy? It's not the only fertile, geographically varied country in Europe, or the only one with a rich gastronomic tradition. It's obviously not the only one whose food tastes good to us. Our ineluctable attraction to Italian food is almost certainly related at least partly to the generosity, of both spirit and actual victuals, with which it is so frequently presented—to its fabled *abbondanza*, its glorious, shameless abundance (the very quality, incidentally, that has always made Italy's

Delivering chianti in straw-wrapped *fiaschi*, or flasks, in Florence in the 1930s, right.

attempts at "nuova cucina", or nouvelle cuisine, seem to us so prissy and so hollow). It could be something about purity of presentation, too—identifiability of ingredients, lack of artifice—or, if you want to get psychological about it, about the way Italy, more than any other country, took so many of our continent's archetypal native flavors—tomatoes most of all, but also peppers, beans, zucchini, even potatoes—and gave them back to us in far more savory form. Or maybe it's just that, whether we grew up eating burgers or tamales or rice with pickled vegetables, Italian food—and, most likely, pasta specifically—gave us our first taste of something really new and our introduction to the universally appealing flavors of the Mediterranean (a sea, it might be pointed out, that Italy doesn't just border but extends down into and is literally defined by).

Not that the Italian food we knew when we were younger is much like the Italian food we eat today. Acres have been written on the subject of Italian-American cooking. We've long since learned that it is poor people's home cooking uncomfortably adapted to the restaurant table; that it has nothing to do with the way people really eat

Boys carrying racks of pasta into the sun to dry, left, probably in southern Italy, in 1929.

PASTA

F orget the old routine about Marco Polo discovering noodles in China and bringing them back to his Italian homeland. The Greeks, located far more conveniently, just across the eastern Adriatic from Italy, were making noodles long before Polo was born (and, anyway, some revisionist historians now doubt that Polo ever got to China in the first place). In its purest form, pasta—literally, "paste"—is nothing more than flour mixed with water or eggs (and occasionally

both), then cut or shaped into various forms, and usually dried at least a little and sometimes a lot. In its earliest days all pasta was probably fresh, made more or less to order. By the 13th century, if not before, however, dried pasta—made from glutinous durum wheat (*Triticum turgidum*) and with water, not eggs, thus giving it a long shelf life—had become both a gastronomic commonplace and an article of trade. (Raw wheat and flour are perishable commodities, but they could be turned into noodles and transported even across the seas.) The surprising thing is that until the 20th century, pasta wasn't an important part of the daily diet for many Italians—especially in the poorer regions of northern Italy, where the main sources of starch were more likely to be chestnuts, polenta, or rice. Today, of course, pasta is immediately and inedelibly associated with Italian cooking in the public consciousness. And today, of course, Italians from every corner of the country take their pasta very seriously. There is even now a full-fledged pasta museum in Rome.

TOMATOES

By now, everybody surely knows that tomatoes, the vegetable most vividly associated with Italian cuisine (garlic is its only real competition), are not an ancient Mediterranean vegetable but a post-Columbian gift to Europe from the New World. What may not be such common knowledge is that the tomato (called pomodoro, or golden apple, in Italian, suggesting that yellow tomatoes may have been known before red ones) didn't start showing up on the peninsula in 1493—and in fact remained a comparative rarity on the Italian table until the 19th century. True, the first published recipe for pasta with tomato sauce in Italy appeared in 1692—but outside the fertile south, where tomatoes grow so freely that whole landscapes turn tomato-red in summer—the

fruit didn't really take hold throughout Italy until the early 1900s, when *conservati*, or canned tomatoes, first became widely available. Today, fresh, juicy, ripe tomatoes are greatly prized in Italy in season, especially for sauces and in soups and stews, but it is worth noting that Italians tend to prefer their salad tomatoes slightly underripe; that those sun-dried tomatoes that have become so popular in America are mostly a specialty product in Italy, primarily in Liguria and Campania, where they are seldom used when fresh tomatoes are in season; and that canned tomatoes continue to be extremely popular in Italian kitchens—especially the exquisite san marzanos (above) of Campania, which are widely considered to be the finest of all cooking tomatoes, perhaps even preferable to fresh (see page 90).

in Italy; that it isn't "authentic". Leaving aside the question of the accuracy of these statements (leaving aside, for instance, the matter of the vitality and, yes, the authenticity of the traditional cooking we've discovered in Italian communities in places like San Francisco, St. Louis, and New York City—all of them represented in the following pages), we can certainly admit that our view of Italian food was, to put it mildly, somewhat limited. With occasional exceptions (Ligurian and Piedmontese dishes in San Francisco; a slight flavor of Lombardy in St. Louis), the things we ate at Casa Mario and Luigi's and Stella di Mare 20 or 30 years ago were most likely Neapolitan or Sicilian in origin. Venice was a travel poster. Florence was art museums. We'd never heard of Friuli or Le Marche or Puglia. All we knew about eating in Rome was that lions used to do it to Christians.

Now look at us. Pasta—not just spaghetti and "macaroni" (our rendering of *maccheroni*) but capellini, fusilli, and lasagnette—has become part of our national repertoire. Olive oil, most of it at least putatively Italian, is our cooking (and salad dressing) medium of choice, and we can now buy great parmigiano, great prosciutto, an encyclopedia of

A farm woman, circa 1950, winnows big handfuls of grain on a hillside in Puglia, right.

pasta, right here at our neighborhood markets. We eat ciabatta and focaccia and bruschetta as casually as our parents once ate Wonder bread. We cool ourselves with gelato and granita and warm ourselves with ribollita and osso buco. We pour balsamic vinegar over everything, like ketchup. We sip pinot grigio in place of chardonnay and blow C-notes on barolo. And we go with seemingly endless enthusiasm to restaurants that promise, and sometimes deliver, the real food of almost every region of Italy.

That last part is important, because along the way we've begun to learn at least part of the incredibly rich Italian culinary vocabulary. We've discovered that Italy has not one cuisine but many—that the Moorish-inflected dishes of southern Sicily and the Austrian-accented specialties of the Alto Adige, for instance, are as different from one another as…well, the rich cream-and-butter sauces of Piedmont are from the spicy oil-and-tomato sauces of Lazio. And we've also learned enough to realize that restaurants—however much we may enjoy them—are only part of the story; that the best Italian food, the dishes that define it most memorably and the ones we're really thinking of when we fantasize

Two men and a boy pause while pruning olive trees, somewhere in southern Italy, in 1894, left.

OLIVE OIL

In Italy, olive oil is not, as a rule, poured into tiny plates and served at the table instead of butter. (This is mostly an American affectation, anyway.) It is the lubricant of culinary life, used for dressing salads, vegetables, cold fish, and more; for preserving mushrooms, anchovies, tuna, certain cheeses, and almost anything else worth saving for later; for deep-frying, shallow-frying, sautéing; as shortening in breads and pastries; even sometimes as medicine. Although olive

oil is consumed more in the center and south of Italy and along the coastline than in the heart of the north, it is revered even in Piedmont and Lombardy, the realm of butter and pork fat. Unlike grapevines, which grow almost everywhere in Italy, olive trees, those ghostly gray-green heraldic emblems of Mediterranean life, are climatically particular. They flourish in the sunny south, especially in Puglia, Calabria, and Sicily, struggle successfully in Tuscany, and manage to produce delicate oil in small quantities in Liguria, around Lake Garda, in Sardinia, and near Trieste. Although the oils of the south have improved mightily in quality in recent years, and although Liguria oil has its fierce partisans, most connoisseurs seem to think that the top Tuscan oils, peppery and full flavored (and often produced by good Tuscan wine estates), are the best of all. But be careful: Italy is the world's largest consumer of olive oil and second-largest producer (after Spain), but also the world's largest importer. At least some "Italian" olive oil, even that with Tuscan-sounding names, comes from Spain, Greece, or North Africa.

PROSCIUTTO

The word *prosciutto* (derived from the verb *prosciugare*, to dry) simply means ham—any kind of ham, even the soft pink cooked stuff. What we (and the Italians themselves) commonly call just prosciutto is actually prosciutto crudo, raw (but cured) ham. The most famous prosciutto of this kind bears the appellation "di Parma", meaning that, while it may be made from the meat of pigs raised in Lombardy, Piedmont, or the Veneto as well as Emilia-Romagna, it must be cured in the last region and, specifically, in the province of Parma. At its best, prosciutto di Parma (right) is rosy hued and silky in texture, with a vaguely spicy aroma and a faintly salty, earthy-sweet flavor. Eaten by itself or with ripe melon or figs, or used judi-

ciously in cooking (see pages 106 and 214, for instance), it is one of Italy's great culinary treats. A refinement on this already refined product is culatello, sometimes called the filet mignon of prosciutto. Made not from the entire haunch of the pig but only from the posterior muscle (i.e., the buttocks), it is lower in fat than regular prosciutto, subtler in flavor, and of course more expensive. Other parts of Italy make highly regarded prosciutto, too, among them Alta Irpinia, Carpegna, Casentino, Norcia, and Sauris—but Parma's only full-scale rival for ham supremacy is San Daniele, in the Friuli region. Cured on the hoof, unlike Parma prosciutto, the ham of San Daniele tends to be moister, more delicate, and slightly more salty.

about our next Italian meal, are *cucina casalinga*—home cooking. Which is why, as the editors of SAVEUR, we keep getting on those trains and boats and planes and going off to find it where it lives, to meet the people who create it today and whose ancestors invented it—and we don't look just in restaurants and trattorias, either. We log countless hours in home kitchens, in the fields with farmers, on the docks waiting for the fishermen to come in. We drive up into the hills of Liguria to watch a housewife fashioning little corkscrew gnocchi by hand; we help a dapper hotelier prepare tripe for lunch in his elegant villa on the edge of a Venetian canal; we follow an American-born actor as he traces the footsteps of his grandfather, a *monzù*, or master chef, in a small Sicilian mountain village; we learn how to make risotto—and find out why it has to be made that way—from the most celebrated Italian cooking teacher of our time; back home, we even duck into a social club in San Francisco's Little Italy to watch an "old stove" mix up a salt cod salad. Then, more ravenous than ever for Italian food, we bring it all back home. —COLMAN ANDREWS, *Editor,* SAVEUR

On a street in Rocca di Papa, in Lazio, in 1954, a woman sells pork products, right.

ANTIPASTI AND SALADS

"IT WAS at Casale, an ancient inn on the

via Flaminia, one of those famous roads

that lead to Rome, that I discovered real

Italian antipasto—not some platter of cold

meats but a veritable groaning board of cold vegetables, marinated, grilled, or meat-and-rice stuffed; fresh ricotta and bufala mozzarella; a variety of olives, salami, and anchovies. It seemed like all of Italy's bounty on one two-tiered table." —COLMAN ANDREWS

Pomodori a Riso

(Tomatoes Stuffed with Rice)

SERVES 4–8

STUFFED VEGETABLES appear on nearly every antipasto table in Italy. These rice-filled tomatoes are part of the regular (immense) selection at Casale on the via Flaminia.

8 *firm, ripe medium tomatoes*
½ cup raw arborio or other risotto rice
2 tbsp. finely chopped fresh Italian parsley
2 tbsp. finely chopped fresh basil
2 cloves garlic, peeled and minced
½ cup extra-virgin olive oil
Salt and freshly ground black pepper

1. Position oven rack in top third of oven, then preheat oven to 400°. Pull stems off tomato tops, then trim about ¾" from bottom of each tomato and set ends aside. Working over a medium bowl, use a small spoon to carefully scoop out inner pulp without puncturing the walls of the tomatoes. Reserve scooped-out pulp. Arrange scooped-out tomatoes open end up in a medium baking dish.

2. Pass tomato pulp through a food mill or pulse in the bowl of a food processor to a chunky purée, then transfer back into bowl. Add rice, parsley, basil, garlic, and oil, then season generously with salt and pepper. Mix well. Spoon filling into prepared tomatoes (there may be a little filling left over) and place a reserved tomato end loosely on top of each stuffed tomato. Drizzle a little oil over tomatoes and bake until rice is swollen and tender and tomatoes are soft and well browned, about 50 minutes. Remove from oven and set aside to let cool to room temperature.

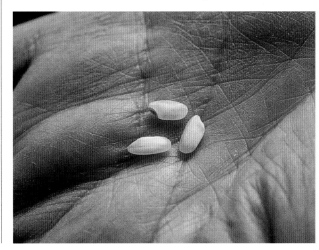

Road Food

Casale, on the via Flaminia, just outside Rome, dates back to at least the 18th century, when it was a roadside inn welcoming (and feeding) travelers from afar. Today, it's a taxi ride from the centro but is no less appreciated by hungry visitors. The antipasto table is an epic array of vegetables, meats, cheeses, and more. The pasta—displayed in big ivory-hued curls near the antipasto—is homemade and served with basic, well-made sauces based on things like porcini mushrooms, squash blossoms, and cooked-down meat. The biggest attraction here, though, might be the roast pork and lamb, cooked continuously on a massive rotisserie to the side of one portion of the dining room. And almost as tasty as the succulent, salty meat itself are the potatoes cooked in the dripping fat at the rotisserie's bottom. Casale used to be a good place to stop while traveling; now it's worth a trip.

Precious Blossoms

From the moment they arrive at market stands in the early morning hours, in late spring and early summer, yellow-orange squash flowers (often from zucchini but also from pumpkin and other members of the genus *Cucurbita*) are a precious commodity. At farmers' markets in the United States, in fact, you might have to ask for them, since they're often hidden in coolers to protect them from the morning heat. When buying squash blossoms, look for examples that are firm, not wilted, and nicely inflated, with the green veins extended and the bud slightly open. Because squash blossoms are extremely perishable, it's best to cook them the same day you buy them—and if the weather is warm, emulate those market sellers: keep the blossoms crisp by storing them in the refrigerator until you're ready to use them.

Fiori di Zucca Ripieni
(Stuffed and Fried Squash Blossoms)

SERVES 6

ZUCCHINI and other squash blossoms are fried—stuffed or not—all over Italy. This recipe comes from Antico Ristorante Pagnanelli in Castel Gandolfo, in the hills near Rome.

¾ *lb. fresh mozzarella, diced*
12 *anchovy filets, coarsely chopped*
24 *blossoms of zucchini or other squash, stamens removed*
4 *eggs*
2 *cups flour*
Freshly ground black pepper
Vegetable oil
Salt

1. Mix together mozzarella and anchovies in a medium bowl. Stuff each zucchini blossom with the mixture and gently twist petals shut so that the stuffing won't leak out during cooking.

2. Beat eggs in a small bowl. Pour 1 cup flour into a shallow pan. In a second shallow pan, season the remaining 1 cup of flour with pepper. Pour oil into a heavy skillet to a depth of 3". Heat oil over high heat until hot but not smoking, about 375° on a candy thermometer. (If oil isn't hot enough, squash blossoms will absorb too much of it.) Working in small batches, dredge each stuffed blossom in flour; dip into egg wash, turning to coat well; then dredge in seasoned flour. Fry blossoms in batches, turning frequently, until crisp, 3–5 minutes. Drain on paper towels, sprinkle with salt, and serve immediately.

Bagna Cauda

(Raw Vegetables with Warm Anchovy–Garlic Sauce)

SERVES 8

IN PIEDMONT, winemakers celebrate the end of the grape harvest each year with a dinner that begins with bagna cauda (literally, "warm bath") and ends, according to tradition, with eggs scrambled in the last traces of the sauce.

½ cup butter
10 cloves garlic, peeled
  and thinly sliced
24 oil-packed anchovies,
  chopped
2 cups extra-virgin
  olive oil
Salt and freshly ground
  black pepper
4 stalks cardoon, washed
Juice of 1 lemon
4–6 lbs. assorted raw
  vegetables, at least 4
  varieties—for instance,
  fennel, baby artichokes,
  Belgian endive, carrots,
  radicchio, and celery—
  washed, trimmed, and
  cut into pieces

1. Melt butter in a small saucepan over low heat. Add garlic and cook until soft, about 3 minutes. Add anchovies and drizzle in olive oil. Cook over low heat, crushing anchovies slightly with a fork and stirring until flavors are blended, 10–15 minutes. Season with salt and pepper and keep warm.

2. Carefully cut thorns and leaves off cardoon stalks, then peel with a swivel vegetable peeler (right). Cut cardoons into pieces 3"–4" long and put into a medium bowl with lemon juice and water to cover.

3. To serve, arrange vegetables on a platter and put anchovy–garlic sauce into a warm bowl so that each diner can dip vegetables into the sauce.

Wealthy Man's Treat

A member of the thistle family and ancestor of the globe artichoke, the cardoon (*Cynara cardunculus*), usually considered essential for a bagna cauda, has been growing in southern Europe and North Africa for centuries. Pliny supposedly called cardoons a wealthy man's treat; the farmers of medieval Córdoba and Carthage turned them into big business; and they were apparently cultivated in the Moorish gardens of Seville. In 1911, British culinary historian Frederick Hackwood described the cardoon as "a delicacy of the Italians in former times", suggesting that it had fallen out of favor on the peninsula. Perhaps it was once more widely consumed in some regions than it is today, but it remains a favorite in Sicily, Tuscany, Piedmont, and Abruzzo.

Radicchio Americano

When Lucio Gomiero, one of America's major radicchio growers—with farms in Salinas and Bakersfield, California, as well as Florida ("between," as he says, "the sugarcane and the alligators"), Arizona, and even Quebec—invited us to his house in Monterey County for a home-cooked meal, we naturally expected that radicchio would be included in a course or two. What we didn't expect was that it would either be, or be in, virtually *every* course—grilled, sautéed with garlic and olive oil, as tempura, in salad, canapés, pizza, pasta, and two versions of a classic Italian soup—or that it would prove to be so versatile and adaptable that we didn't grow tired of it for an instant. "One way or another," says Gomiero, "I eat radicchio every day." When he and his family first moved to California from Italy's Veneto region, he recalls, his children—Camilla, Giulia, and Giacomo, now 13, 15, and 19, respectively—used to complain about the inevitability of radicchio at the family table. "I used to tell them," says Gomiero, "'No radicchio, no America!'"

Radicchio di Treviso Marinato

(Marinated Radicchio di Treviso)

SERVES 4

CALIFORNIA-BASED radicchio grower Lucio Gomiero, who sells about 24 million heads of the chicory a year, mostly in America, discovered this dish at Trattoria da Mario in Montegrotto Terme, near his family home in Padua.

6 heads radicchio
  di treviso
1 cup white wine vinegar
5 black peppercorns
Salt
1 bay leaf
½ cup extra-virgin
  olive oil
Freshly ground black
  pepper
1 hard-cooked egg, finely
  grated

1. Remove and discard any imperfect outer leaves from radicchio, then quarter heads lengthwise and set aside. Combine vinegar, 3 cups water, peppercorns, ½ tsp. salt, and bay leaf in a large pot and bring to a boil. Blanch radicchio wedges, a few at a time, for 1–2 minutes. Blot dry with a kitchen towel, squeezing gently to remove as much moisture as possible.

2. Arrange wedges in layers in a glass or ceramic dish. Drizzle with olive oil, cover with plastic wrap, and refrigerate overnight. (Radicchio will keep, refrigerated, for up to 2 weeks.) To serve, bring radicchio to room temperature, season with salt and black pepper, and slice (radicchio may also be served unsliced). Garnish with grated egg.

Puntarelle con Salsa di Acciughe

(Puntarelle with Anchovy Dressing)

SERVES 4

IN SOME parts of Italy, people think puntarelle are weeds—but not in the countryside around Rome, a city where this chicory has become a much anticipated winter tradition.

1 head puntarelle
4 anchovy filets
1 clove garlic, peeled
2 tbsp. fresh lemon juice
2 tbsp. extra-virgin olive oil
Freshly ground black pepper

1. Wash puntarelle and remove any bruised outer leaves. With a paring knife, split the stalks lengthwise. Place puntarelle strips into a large bowl of ice water and soak for 30 minutes. (Strips will become crisp and slightly curled.) Drain and set aside.

2. With a mortar and pestle, grind anchovy filets and garlic into a paste, then transfer to a large bowl and whisk in lemon juice and olive oil. Toss puntarelle with the dressing until leaves are evenly coated. Season generously with pepper.

Winter Bitter

Every year, when the markets start filling with sturdy winter vegetables, Romans turn to puntarelle. A member of the genus *Cichorium* (an extensive clan that also includes endive and radicchio), puntarelle (literally, "little points") come into season in November and are available through February. Each head is about a foot long, with a healthy fringe of feathery green leaves—but these are too bitter for most tastes. The prize is the cluster of hollow white stalks from which the leaves grow. These are bitter, too, but their bitterness is tempered by soaking in ice water, and they seem to turn almost sweet. In folk medicine, puntarelle are supposed to be good for the stomach and for purifying the blood. They also do wonders for the palate.

Blood Oranges

As the golden morning light of winter washes over la fiera, the daily market in the eastern Sicilian city of Catania," writes fruit expert David Karp, "shoppers bustle between stalls piled high with arance sanguigne—blood oranges—some cut in half to reveal their ruby or dark violet flesh. And the blood oranges are not just in the market. All over town, from the backs of three-wheeled trucks, weathered vendors cry 'Dolcissimi!'— 'The sweetest!'—in praise of the best blood orange of all, the tarocco (above). Long after midnight, crowds are still gathered at kiosks, sipping thick vermilion juice blended with mineral water. Here, hot summers bring sweetness to the fruit as it ripens, while cold winter nights, alternating with mild days, favor the development of anthocyanins, the red pigments that give blood oranges their distinctive berrylike taste and color. (Some Italian researchers firmly believe that these anthocyanins strengthen the circulatory system, cure ulcers, and scavenge from the body free radicals that may cause cancer.) Although Italy produces more than 3 billion pounds of blood oranges per year, most farms are under three acres. Connoisseurs insist that the Sicilian arancia sanguigna at its best, with its intense flavor, balance of acidity and sweetness, and complex aftertaste, is the world's finest dessert orange."

Insalata di Arancia Sanguigna e Cipolla Rossa
(Blood Orange and Red Onion Salad)

ITALIANS USUALLY eat blood oranges, which are sold in Italy from January through April every year, plain, in their simply glory, as dessert, or else squeeze them into juice—but this refreshing winter salad is a classic in Sicily.

3–4 blood oranges, peeled, with all pith removed
1 small red onion, peeled, cut into very thin slices, and separated into rings
Salt and freshly cracked black pepper
3–4 tbsp. extra-virgin olive oil

1. Cut oranges into ¼"-thick slices and arrange on a serving platter. Scatter onions over orange slices. Season with salt and pepper to taste and drizzle with oil.

Carpaccio

SERVES 6

ALMOST anything thinly sliced is called "carpaccio" these days, but the original, created in 1950 at Harry's Bar in Venice, was named for its color—that is, for the great Venetian painter Vittorio Carpaccio, who was noted for his reds and whites. The dish, it is said, was invented for a Harry's regular whose doctor forbade her to eat cooked meat.

1 egg yolk
1 tsp. white wine or red wine vinegar
¼ tsp. dry mustard
Salt and freshly ground white pepper
¾ cup vegetable oil
Juice of half a lemon
1–2 dashes Worcestershire sauce or to taste
1½ tsp. milk
1½ lbs. boned, chilled (not frozen) shell steak, trimmed of all fat, sinew, and gristle

1. Make a mayonnaise by putting egg yolk, vinegar, mustard, and a little salt and pepper into a medium mixing bowl and whisking until thoroughly blended. Add ¼ cup of the oil drop by drop, whisking constantly. Gradually add the rest of the oil in a thin, steady stream, continuing to whisk as the mayonnaise thickens. Add 1 tbsp. of the lemon juice, or to taste, and adjust seasonings. If the mayonnaise seems too thick, whisk in a little water (or beef or chicken broth) to thin it.

2. Put ½ cup of the mayonnaise (reserve the rest for another use) into a small mixing bowl; whisk in Worcestershire and ¼ tsp. of the lemon juice, then enough milk to make a thin sauce that just coats the back of a wooden spoon. Season to taste with salt and pepper and add a little more Worcestershire sauce and/or lemon juice, if you like.

3. Making sure the beef is very cold, slice into the thinnest-possible sheets, using a razor-sharp, long-bladed slicing knife. It will probably take several practice tries before you are able to get thin, even slices. Divide slices between 6 small chilled plates, arranging them in one thin layer, covering the surface of the plates completely. Drizzle some of the sauce over meat on each plate and serve immediately.

Another Artist

The second-most famous creation of Harry's Bar, after carpaccio, is almost certainly an elegant cocktail named for another Italian artist—the Bellini. To make two Bellinis, combine 2 oz. (¼ cup) very cold white peach purée with 6 oz. (¾ cup) ice-cold prosecco (sparkling wine from the Veneto), then pour into two small chilled tumblers. When white peaches are in season, you may want to make your own peach purée by passing the pitted peaches through a food mill, then passing the purée through a sieve. "Never use yellow peaches, and never purée the peaches by machine," says Arrigo Cipriani, proprietor of Harry's Bar—although Harry's itself now makes its Bellinis, year-round, with La Fruitière du Val Evel brand frozen white peach purée (available in some specialty food stores in the United States). It may be heresy, incidentally, but we've also had very good Bellinis made not with prosecco but with good old-fashioned nonvintage champagne.

Surf 'n' Turf

Ask for vitello tonnato in most Italian restaurants in America, and you'll get thin slices of cold poached veal topped with tuna-thickened mayonnaise with a couple of capers on top. It's not a bad dish as long as the veal's not too dry—but, complains Marcella Hazan, who knows (and teaches) more about Italian food than anybody else in America, it's not the real thing. True vitello tonnato, says Hazan (below, with husband Victor Hazan), is made with alternating layers of thinly sliced veal and rich, creamy tuna sauce, left overnight so the flavors can marry. "The sauce must impregnate the veal to the point that it's impossible to detect where the veal ends and the sauce starts," she adds. Oh, and don't try to make this dish with fresh tuna. "Use imported tuna that's packed in olive oil," Hazan counsels. "It's expensive, but the intensity of the olive oil is essential." Hazan makes her vitello tonnato a day in advance and serves it as a main course in summer or as an elegant antipasto any time of year.

Vitello Tonnato
(Cold Veal with Tuna Sauce)

SERVES 6–8

THIS DISH of "tuna'ed" veal, which will improve for as long as a week in the refrigerator, was probably invented in Lombardy or Piedmont, both famous for their veal specialties.

FOR VEAL:
2½ lbs. lean veal roast, preferably top round, tightly trussed
1 medium carrot, peeled and chopped
1 rib celery, without leaves, chopped
1 medium yellow onion, peeled and chopped
4 sprigs fresh Italian parsley
1 bay leaf

FOR TUNA SAUCE:
1 7-oz. can olive oil–packed tuna
5 anchovy filets
1 cup extra-virgin olive oil
1 tbsp. fresh lemon juice
3 tbsp. capers, soaked and rinsed
1¼ cups mayonnaise

1. For veal, put veal into a deep, heavy pan. Add carrot, celery, onion, parsley, bay leaf, and enough water to cover. Remove meat and set it aside. Cover pan, bring water to a boil over high heat, then return veal to pan. Return to a boil, cover, reduce heat to low, and gently simmer for 2 hours. Add more water if necessary. Remove pan from heat, set aside, and allow meat to cool in the stock.

2. For sauce, drain tuna and put into the bowl of a food processor fitted with a metal blade. Add anchovies, oil, lemon juice, and capers and process until it becomes a creamy, beige-colored sauce. Fold sauce gently but thoroughly into mayonnaise. If making ahead of time, refrigerate.

3. When meat is cool, transfer to a cutting board. Remove trussing strings and carefully cut into uniformly thin slices.

4. Spread some of the tuna sauce on bottom of a platter. Over it, lay a single layer of veal slices, edge to edge, without overlapping, then cover them with sauce. Repeat process until all veal slices are used up, ending with a layer of sauce.

5. Cover platter with plastic wrap and refrigerate for at least 24 hours. (It will keep for at least a week.) Bring to room temperature before serving. Use a spatula to smooth the top. Garnish with thin lemon slices, slivered black olives, whole capers, whole Italian parsley leaves, and/or anchovy filets, if you like.

Fresh Isn't Everything

P reserved fish has always been an essential part of the Mediterranean diet. Anchovies, sardines, and tuna, among other fish, have been packed in salt or submerged in olive oil for many centuries. The roe of tuna and gray mullet has been dried and salted (the Italians call this bottarga) for almost as long as sailors have plied the sea. Cod from far northern waters, either dried or salted, became a major item of trade in the region centuries ago (see page 181). In earlier times, preserving fish was a practical matter—the Mediterranean yields comparatively little fresh fish in the first place, and before refrigeration there was no efficient way to store and transport it anyway—but a taste for these items has long since become part of the culture, in Italy and elsewhere. When an Italian recipe calls for canned tuna, then, don't substitute fresh; the oil-packed stuff (above) is more authentic.

Tonno e Fagioli

(Tuna and White Bean Salad)

SERVES 6

VENTRESCA, or tuna belly, packed in olive oil, is best for this dish, but any good olive oil–packed tuna will do. Don't use water-packed tuna; the results will taste insipid.

4 cups cooked white beans (see page 75, step 1)
2 7-oz. cans olive oil–packed ventresca or other olive oil–packed tuna, lightly drained
1 small red onion, peeled and thinly sliced
Extra-virgin olive oil
Salt and freshly ground black pepper

1. Place beans in a large serving bowl and add tuna. Break up the tuna into large chunks with a wooden spoon. Scatter onions over tuna, then drizzle with olive oil and season generously with salt and pepper.

Papa Was a Monzù

My father died when I was three," remembers Vincent Schiavelli (above), protean actor, television personality, and cookbook author, "and my grandparents Papa Andrea and Carolina took us to live with them in their very loving, very Sicilian home in Brooklyn." Every afternoon, as Schiavelli did his schoolwork at one end of the kitchen table, Papa Andrea—who had been trained in the Sicilian village of Polizzi Generosa as a *monzù*, or master chef (the word is a corruption of *monsieur*, because the noble houses of 19th-century Sicily and Naples originally had French chefs)—would prepare dinner at the other. "When my assignments were done," Schiavelli continues, "I would help him with simple tasks— peeling, mixing, stirring—and he would tell me about Sicily and about his early days in America at the turn of the century. Over the years, I learned much about his life and just as much about cooking."

Funci Chini
(Sicilian Stuffed Mushrooms)

SERVES 6–8

ONE OF the many specialties Papa Andrea Coco brought to America from his native Sicily and taught to his grandson was this unusual version of stuffed mushrooms.

18 *large white mushrooms*
  (about 2 lbs.)
Extra-virgin olive oil
Salt
¼ *cup marsala*
1½ *cups fresh bread*
  crumbs
1 *cup grated pecorino*
  romano
2 *tbsp. finely chopped fresh*
  Italian parsley
1 *clove garlic, peeled and*
  minced
Freshly ground black
  pepper

1. Preheat oven to 375°. Remove and coarsely chop stems from mushrooms, reserving caps. Heat 3 tbsp. oil in a large, deep, nonstick skillet over medium-high heat. Add chopped mushrooms, season with salt, and cook, stirring occasionally, until mushroom mixture is dry, about 5 minutes. Slowly add marsala. Cook until marsala has evaporated, about 2 minutes, then remove from heat and stir in bread crumbs. Set aside to let cool, then add pecorino, parsley, and garlic. Mix thoroughly.

2. Place mushroom caps in a single layer (rounded side down) on a greased cookie sheet. Spoon mushroom filling into caps, drizzle with oil, season with pepper, and bake until golden, 30–45 minutes. Serve warm.

Panzanella

(Tuscan Tomato and Bread Salad)

SERVES 4

DON'T BOTHER making this traditional Tuscan appetizer unless you can get delicious, vine-ripened seasonal tomatoes. Bland, cottony tomatoes yield mediocre panzanella.

¾ cup extra-virgin
    olive oil
3 cloves garlic, peeled and
    sliced
Half a baguette or some
    good country-style
    bread, cut into ½" cubes
3–4 lbs. tomatoes (use
    several varieties,
    if possible)
2 tbsp. red wine vinegar
Salt
1 handful fresh basil
    leaves, thinly sliced

1. Preheat oven to 350°. Heat about half the oil in a large, ovenproof skillet over medium heat, then remove skillet from heat, add garlic and bread cubes, and mix well. Place skillet in oven and bake until bread cubes are golden and crisp, 10–15 minutes. Remove skillet from oven and set aside to let cool.

2. Meanwhile, prepare the tomatoes. If using cherry tomatoes, remove stems and slice in half. For larger tomatoes, core and slice into medium cubes. Put tomatoes into a large bowl, add vinegar and remaining oil, then season to taste with salt, mix well, and set aside.

3. Shortly before serving, toss bread and basil with the tomatoes. Divide panzanella evenly between 4 shallow soup bowls. Garnish with sprigs of basil, if you like.

Bread Again

T raditional Italian bread, whether rough-textured country style or the light white-fleshed variety, is made without preservatives and so hardens quickly. This does not pose a problem in the Italian kitchen: when bread is fresh and soft, it is eaten as bread; when it grows firm, it gets turned into mollica, or toasted bread crumbs, to be sprinkled on pasta (especially in Sicily) as a poor folks' substitute for grated cheese, or it gets mixed into salads (like panzanella) or soups (e.g., Tuscany's ribollita; see page 75) or something between the two (most notably pappa al pomodoro; see page 80).

Seafarer's Fare

For centuries, Genoa has been wealthy, cosmopolitan, and well fed. It became a commercial and maritime center in the 11th century and grew into a powerful commune with a budding rivalry with Pisa and Venice. By the 12th century it had transformed itself into an independent republic with a population of 100,000 (today, it exceeds 600,000) and, by the 13th, into a major capital of banking and trade. In the centuries that followed, Genoa developed a number of complicated local dishes, primarily because it could afford to—and also probably just because it had access, through its widespread trade, to ingredients and culinary notions from many parts of the world. It's also possible that the republic's dependence on its trading fleet inspired ornate dishes: its sailors traveled such great distances that their homecomings were events to be celebrated, especially with gastronomic set pieces like cappon magro (literally, "thin capon"; traditionally, the term *magro* identified a meatless dish suitable for days of religious fast or abstinence)—a dish that must have seemed very special indeed to a vegetable-deprived sailor just home from months upon the waves.

Cappon Magro
(Genoese Fish and Vegetable Salad)

SERVES 8–10

SHIP'S biscuits, or hardtack—gallette marinare in Italian—are an ancient Mediterranean staple, eaten by sailors from many lands. Look for them in Italian specialty stores.

3 ship's biscuits, halved
5 cloves garlic, peeled;
   1 whole, 4 minced
1 cup red wine vinegar
Salt
3 large carrots, peeled
1 medium zucchini
2 medium potatoes, peeled
2 medium beets, peeled
½ lb. green beans, trimmed
½ head cauliflower, cored
10 baby artichokes
1 ¾ cups extra-virgin
   olive oil
Freshly ground black pepper
10 large shrimp, unpeeled
1 2-lb. cod filet
4 slices country-style
   Italian bread, ½"
   thick, crusts removed
2 cups packed fresh Italian
   parsley leaves
2 tbsp. pine nuts
6 hard-cooked eggs; 5 whole,
   1 sliced
20 oil-packed anchovy
   filets, drained and
   finely chopped
¼ cup large capers, drained
10 green or black olives,
   pitted
10 oil-packed baby
   mushrooms
10 pickled cherry peppers
10 fresh oysters, on half shell

1. Rub the cut side of each ship's biscuit with a whole garlic clove. Place biscuits on a platter and sprinkle with ¼ cup of the vinegar and ½ cup water.

2. Bring a large pot of salted water to a boil over high heat. Trim and cut carrots, zucchini, potatoes, and beets into ½"-thick slices; cut green beans into thirds; divide cauliflower into florets; trim and quarter artichokes. Cook each separately (beginning with artichokes and ending with beets) until tender. Drain and refresh in cold water as cooked. Keeping vegetables separate, dress them with 1 generous tbsp. each of vinegar and oil. Season with salt and pepper.

3. Bring a medium pot of salted water to a boil. Add shrimp and cook until pink and firm, 1–2 minutes. Drain and set aside. Place cod in a large skillet, add enough water to cover, season with salt, and bring just to a simmer over medium heat, cooking until fish flakes, 12–15 minutes. Drain, cool, flake, and dress with oil and vinegar. Set aside.

4. Place bread in a bowl, add 2 tbsp. vinegar and ¼ cup water, and set aside until liquid is absorbed. Transfer to a food processor. Add remaining garlic, parsley, pine nuts, yolks from 3 of the eggs (coarsely chop the whites and set them aside), one-third of the anchovies, half of the capers, and ¾ cup water. Purée until smooth, then drizzle in 1 cup of the oil. Add more water if green sauce is too thick.

5. To assemble, spread remaining anchovies on ship's biscuits and top with alternating layers of vegetables (one kind per layer) and cod (about 3 layers total). Spread a bit of green sauce over each layer of cod; insert sliced egg and chopped white midway through. Layer until all ingredients are used up, finishing with potatoes. Spread more green sauce on top. Quarter remaining 3 eggs and use as garnish, along with shrimp, olives, mushrooms, peppers, and oysters.

North Beach

L ife in North Beach, the colorful old Italian neighborhood of San Francisco, is perfumed by food, driven by food, about food. With the possible exception of New York's Little Italy, North Beach is the most famous Italian quarter in America. (It was here that the nation's first Columbus Day parade was held, back in 1869.) Italian immigrants started arriving in San Francisco in substantial numbers in the late 19th century. Many of these pioneers came from the northern regions of Piedmont and Liguria and especially the port city of Genoa, reports writer Peggy Knickerbocker, a longtime North Beach resident. And because many of them were fishermen, they naturally settled near the wharves at the end of Columbus Avenue. (There was a beach here once, but it was gradually buried under landfill, beginning in 1849.) By the turn of the century, a thriving community had grown up around what is now Fisherman's Wharf, with cooks setting up tables to sell fresh-caught crab and sourdough bread to the fishermen and their customers. Before long, the area was chockablock with family-style Italian places, and the non-Italian world adopted North Beach as a favorite neighborhood.

Insalata di Baccalà

(Salt Cod Salad)

SERVES 4

SALT COD comes from the North Atlantic but is a basic ingredient in traditional Italian cuisine, in North Beach as in Italy itself. We learned how to make this salad from Joe Delgado, an "old stove"—North Beach slang for someone who has put in a lot of cooking time in his or her day.

1 lb. salt cod
1 lb. russet potatoes, peeled and quartered
1 large bunch Italian parsley
1 medium red onion, peeled and chopped
½ cup extra-virgin olive oil
Freshly ground black pepper

1. Soak salt cod in a large pot of water in refrigerator for 36–48 hours, changing water at least 4 times.

2. Drain salt cod, then return to same pot, add water to barely cover, and bring to a boil. Reduce heat to low and poach salt cod until tender enough to pierce easily with a knife, about 20 minutes. Remove salt cod from pot and drain, reserving poaching water, then place fish in a large bowl to let cool slightly. When it is cool enough to handle, pick through it carefully to remove any pieces of bone, cartilage, or skin.

3. Cook potatoes over medium-high heat in reserved poaching water until tender, about 15 minutes. Drain, allow to cool slightly, then add to salt cod in bowl.

4. Wash and trim parsley, discarding stems, then dry and coarsely chop leaves. Add parsley and onion to potatoes and salt cod. Toss carefully (your hands work best, says Joe Delgado), allowing potatoes and fish to break up slightly. Drizzle with oil, season to taste with pepper, and toss again. Serve at room temperature or refrigerate until serving (salad will keep for several days if refrigerated).

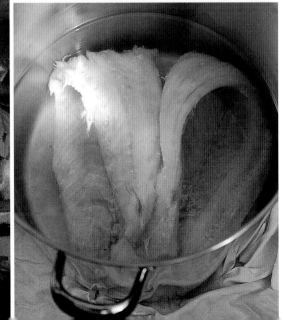

Regional Herbs

O regano may be the herb we associate most often with Italian cooking (see sidebar, page 220), but plenty of others are used freely as well—among them, basil, rosemary, parsley, sage, bay leaf, and thyme. Some herbs seem to appear most often in certain regions, though. Marjoram, or maggiorana (*Majorana hortensis*), is used generously in Liguria, where the oregano-like herb delicately flavors everything from pasta to fish. Pennyroyal, or mentuccia (*Mentha pulegium*), is the favored mint in the Lazio; its small, pungent leaves are considered essential in the classic Roman dish carciofi alla romana (see page 242). Borage, or borragine (*Borago officinalis*), is also popular in Liguria and is commonly used in Campania, especially in lentil dishes. And then there's ginger, zenzero in Italian—not an herb, of course, but a spice, sometimes appearing in traditional Tuscan recipes. But *attenzione*: things are not always what they seem; Tuscans use the term *zenzero* to refer to dried red chiles.

Insalata di Funghi Porcini
(Porcini Salad)

SERVES 4

IN ITALY, mushroom dishes are sometimes flavored with nepitella (*Calamintha nepeta*), or lesser calamint—a wild mint native to southern Europe—as is this simple salad served at Don Lisander in Milan. Some farmers' markets may occasionally carry calamint, and it isn't hard to grow. On the other hand, conventional mint may be substituted.

4 small to medium fresh
  porcini
4 thin slices emmentaler
  cheese
4 small sprigs fresh
  calamint or fresh mint
Salt and freshly ground
  black pepper
Extra-virgin olive oil
8 small leaves frisee lettuce

1. Wipe porcini clean of any dirt with a damp paper towel. Trim off tough ends of stems, then slice porcini very thinly with a sharp, thin-bladed knife. Arrange sliced porcini on 4 plates. Slice cheese into thin strips and arrange over porcini. Coarsely chop calamint leaves and sprinkle over the salad. Season to taste with salt and pepper. Drizzle generously with oil. Garnish with frisee leaves.

Yesterday's Risotto

Chances are you won't have leftovers when you serve risotto—but if you do, you may use it in ways other than arancine:

♦ **RISOTTO CAKES:** Form thin layers of risotto into pancake shapes and fry them in butter until crisp. Sprinkle grated parmigiano over the cakes, if you like.

♦ **SUPPLÌ AL TELEFONO:** These Roman fried rice balls are similar to arancine but are usually filled with only mozzarella—which melts and forms long strings (supposedly resembling telephone lines, which is what the name means) when you take a bite.

♦ **RISOTTO SANDWICHES:** SAVEUR executive editor Christopher Hirsheimer had an Italian friend in San Francisco who used to spread leftover risotto, at room temperature, on sourdough bread for a satisfying sandwich.

Arancine

(Fried Rice Croquettes)

MAKES ABOUT 12

"GOOD arancine can't be eaten too long after they are cooked," says Giovanna Tornabene—whose mother, Wanda, taught us how to make them (left) in the family kitchen in Gangivecchio, in the Sicilian mountains. "Like people, when they sit too long, they grow in weight." *Arancine* means "little oranges"—a reference to the croquettes' shape and color.

FOR RISOTTO:
5–6 cups chicken stock
⅛ tsp. saffron threads, crumbled
3 tbsp. unsalted butter
1½ cups carnaroli or other risotto rice
1 3-oz. piece parmigiano-reggiano rind
1 egg yolk, at room temperature
¼ cup freshly grated parmigiano-reggiano
Salt and freshly ground black pepper

FOR ARANCINE:
3 oz. mozzarella, cut into ½" dice
3 thin slices of cooked ham, cut into ½" squares
2 egg whites, whisked until just foamy
2 cups dried bread crumbs
Sunflower or vegetable oil

1. For risottto, heat stock in a saucepan over medium heat until it just comes to a boil, then reduce heat to low and add saffron.

2. Melt butter in a medium, heavy saucepan over medium heat. Add rice and cook, stirring with a wooden spoon, until rice just begins to turn translucent, about 2 minutes. Add parmigiano rind, then add ¾ cup of the simmering stock, stirring the rice constantly until almost all of the liquid has been absorbed. Add another ¾ cup stock and continue cooking and adding broth (you may have some broth left over) until rice is cooked but firm to the bite, about 20 minutes. Remove and discard rind, stir in egg yolk and parmigiano, and season to taste with salt and pepper. Pour risotto onto a baking sheet to let cool.

3. For arancine, dampen hands with water and divide cooled risotto into loose balls, each measuring about ⅓ cup. One at a time, flatten risotto balls in the palm of one hand. Place 2 cubes of mozzarella and a piece of ham in the center of each, then work the rice to enclose filling completely. Shape each risotto ball into a 3" oval. Dip arancine into whisked egg whites, then roll in bread crumbs. Refrigerate on a baking sheet for 30 minutes.

4. Pour oil into a large, deep-sided frying pan to a depth of 2". Heat over medium heat to a temperature of 325° on a candy thermometer. Working in batches, gently lower arancine into hot oil with a slotted spoon and fry until golden brown, turning arancine often, 2–3 minutes. Drain on paper towels and serve immediately.

Sweet and Round

Small, flat, almost saucer shaped, the sweet and delicate little onions called cipolline (the word literally *means* "little onions"—they measure only about an inch or two in diameter) are popular in Italy, historically during the winter months. They're eaten mostly as antipasto, either glazed in butter, with or without sugar (whose assistance they rarely need), pickled with herbs and spices, or marinated in agrodolce, or sweet and sour sauce (above). When selecting cipolline, choose those that are firm, with dry, papery skins; avoid any that have dark spots or green shoots—and if you're not going to cook them immediately, store cipolline in a cool, dark, dry place.

Cipolline in Agrodolce
(Sweet-and-Sour Baby Italian Onions)

SERVES 4–6

FLAT, FLAVORFUL cipolline onions used to be a rarity in America, but are increasingly available today, at farmers' markets and even in supermarkets. If you can't find them, pearl onions may be substituted—but they're really a different creature. This recipe comes from Casale in Rome.

1 lb. cipolline onions
2 tbsp. extra-virgin
* olive oil*
1 tbsp. finely minced
* prosciutto fat*
1 clove garlic, peeled and
* minced*
2 tbsp. sugar
1 bay leaf
½ cup white wine vinegar
½ tsp. salt

1. Place onions in a bowl of cold water for 10 minutes to loosen skins, then peel with a sharp knife, taking care to remove only papery skins and keep the base intact.

2. Finely mince 1 onion and set aside. Heat oil in a heavy skillet, large enough to hold onions in one layer, over medium heat. Add prosciutto fat and stir with a wooden spoon until melted, about 3 minutes. Add garlic and reserved minced onions and cook until soft and translucent, 6–8 minutes.

3. Add whole onions in one layer, then add sugar, bay leaf, vinegar, salt, and 1 cup water. The water should just cover the onions. Bring to a boil, then reduce heat to low and gently simmer until onions are tender but still firm, about 1½ hours. Allow to cool to room temperature in pan juices before serving.

Caponata

(Sicilian Sweet-and-Sour Eggplant)

SERVES 6

PROBABLY a fisherman's or sailor's dish to begin with, caponata—with its healthy dose of vinegar and acidic tomato sauce—keeps well, actually improving in flavor over time.

2 medium to large
    eggplants, trimmed and
    cut into 1" cubes
Coarse salt
6 ribs celery, trimmed and
    cut into 1" pieces
1½ cups extra-virgin
    olive oil
1 medium yellow onion,
    peeled and chopped
1 cup pitted green olives
½ cup salt-packed capers,
    rinsed
2 cups tomato sauce
    (see page 90, steps 1
    and 2)
½ cup white wine
    vinegar
2 tbsp. sugar

1. Put eggplant in a colander, sprinkle with about 3 tbsp. salt, and toss to coat well. Allow to drain for 1 hour to extract water and any bitterness. Rinse eggplant and pat dry with paper towels.

2. Cook celery in a pot of boiling salted water over high heat for 1 minute. Drain and set aside to let cool.

3. Heat 1 cup of the oil in a large, heavy skillet over high heat until hot but not smoking. Fry eggplant in batches until dark golden brown on all sides, 5–8 minutes per batch. Remove fried eggplant from skillet with a slotted spoon, drain on paper towels, and set aside.

4. Pour off and discard oil, wipe out pan with a paper towel, and return pan to medium heat. Add remaining ½ cup oil and sauté onion, stirring with a wooden spoon, until it begins to brown, about 5 minutes. Add reserved celery and cook for a minute more, then add olives, capers, tomato sauce, vinegar, and sugar. Simmer for 5 minutes, then stir in reserved eggplant. Reduce heat to medium-low and continue to cook for 10 minutes more. Remove from heat and set aside to let cool. Cover with plastic wrap and refrigerate for 24 hours before serving. Serve at room temperature.

Market as Opera

I n her book *On Persephone's Island* (Vintage Departures, 1995), Mary Taylor Simeti describes Sicily as "a fun house mirror in which Italy can behold her national traits and faults distorted and exaggerated". That description might also be applied to one of Sicily's great treasures, La Vucciria. This ancient market in Palermo is a brawling, boisterous street opera of serpentine alleys, more like an Arab souk than, say, the pristine Rialto market in Venice. Color is everywhere—the purple of eggplants, the red of peppers and tomatoes, the black and green and lavender of olives, the off-whites of cheeses, the fleshy, ruddy tones of sausages and salamis. Vendors howl; motor scooters career. Antonio Giannusa, who puts up jars of 'strattu, Sicily's famed tomato paste, presses tastes on us, as street sellers ply us with spleen sandwiches. We can't get enough of it.

Real Garlic Bread

T he first time I tasted bruschetta (which, incidentally, is pronounced bruce-ketta, not brew-shedda or suchlike)," writes Colman Andrews, "was in Rome in the early 1970s. Up to that point, like every other American who had ever been to an Italian restaurant in his native land, I thought that garlic bread was a hunk of spongy white loaf soaked in a mixture of butter and

garlic powder, sometimes with grated parmesan (and not parmigiano-reggiano) on top. What I discovered in Rome was garlic bread that was just that: garlic on bread—specifically, good country-style bread, grilled, rubbed with real, live garlic, and drizzled with olive oil. It was a revelation, glorious in its simplicity, and I quickly became an addict." Although Roman bruschetta is usually served plain, here are some Italian ideas for toppings (put about ⅓ cup of topping on each piece of bread after preparing it according to the recipe at right; each recipe below makes enough topping for 10–12 pieces of bread).

◆ TOMATO AND BASIL: Finely dice 4 ripe tomatoes and mix with 3–4 shredded fresh basil leaves, 2 tbsp. extra-virgin olive oil, and 1 tsp. salt.

◆ WHITE BEANS: Drain 3 cups cooked white beans (see page 75, step 1) and season to taste with salt and freshly ground black pepper.

◆ CAVOLO NERO: Bring a large pot of salted water to a boil over high heat. Add the juice of ½ lemon and the leafy greens (not stems) from 2 bunches cavolo nero (black Italian kale) or green kale. Cook until tender, 20–25 minutes, then drain. Heat ½ cup olive oil in a large skillet. Add 1 crushed, peeled garlic clove, then add kale, season to taste with salt and freshly ground black papper, and sauté for 3–4 minutes.

Bruschetta
(Grilled Bread with Olive Oil and Garlic)

SERVES 2

W E L O V E the bruschetta at Sabatini (below), on the piazza Santa Maria in Trastevere. At this Roman landmark, the bread is grilled over hot coals, for a nice, smoky flavor.

2 thick slices of country-style Italian bread
1 clove garlic, peeled
Extra-virgin olive oil
Salt and freshly ground black pepper

1. Grill bread over medium-hot coals (or under a broiler) until browned and slightly charred in places. Remove bread slices from grill, lightly rub garlic to perfume the bread, then drizzle with extra-virgin olive oil. Sprinkle with a little salt and pepper, if you like.

Crostini

(Italian Canapés)

SERVES 6

SIMPLE CANAPÉS or open-face sandwiches like these are popular caffè snacks in Tuscany and elsewhere in Italy. Spread 1 or 2 tablespoons of topping on each piece of toast. Keep leftover toppings covered in the refrigerator.

18–20 thin slices of country white bread, crusts trimmed (if you like), and toasted

FOR LIVER PÂTÉ:
¼ cup extra-virgin olive oil
1 small yellow onion, peeled and minced
1 lb. chicken livers, cleaned
Salt and freshly ground black pepper
1 tbsp. capers, rinsed
1 tsp. anchovy paste
2 tbsp. butter
1 tsp. tomato paste

FOR PORCINI PÂTÉ:
4 oz. dried porcini
¼ cup extra-virgin olive oil
3 cloves garlic, peeled and minced
2 tbsp. chopped fresh Italian parsley
Salt

FOR TOMATO SAUCE:
2 cups tomato sauce (see page 90, steps 1 and 2)

1. For liver pâté, heat oil in a large skillet over medium-high heat, then sauté onions until soft, 7–8 minutes. Add chicken livers, season to taste with salt and pepper, and sauté until livers brown, about 3 minutes. Remove from heat and stir in capers and anchovy paste. Blend to a coarse paste in a blender or food processor. Melt butter in the same skillet, stir in liver paste and tomato paste, and warm briefly, mixing ingredients well. Allow to cool before spreading.

2. For porcini pâté, soak porcini in a small bowl of hot water until soft, about 30 minutes, then drain. Heat oil in a large skillet over medium-high heat, add porcini, garlic, and parsley, and sauté for 5–6 minutes. Salt to taste, then blend to a coarse paste in a blender or food processor. Allow to cool before spreading.

3. For tomato sauce, drain excess liquid from tomato sauce. Allow to cool before spreading.

see page 90, steps 1 and 2

Loaves of Italy

First-time visitors to Italy are sometimes taken aback by the fact that the bread they're most often served in restaurants is white fleshed, brittle crusted, and bland—not at all, in other words, the lusty country loaves we've come to know from the Lombardy-born Il Fornaio chain or other new-style Italian bakeries in America. Such breads do exist in Italy, however; they're just more often found at markets or in rural inns than in urban restaurants. The flat, sometimes slightly smoky-tasting "slipper" bread called ciabatta; the round, brown pane toscano, cousin to France's classic miche; the dense pane siciliano, with its swirl of sesame seeds in its furrowed crust; the crisp Sardinian flatbread called carta da musica ("sheet-music paper") for its thinness; the acrobatic furrowed "x" that is the typical bread of Ferrara—these are the staff of regional Italian life.

2

SOUPS

"MINESTRONE (literally 'big soup'), a specialty of the old port of Genoa, was sold out of small boats that pulled up along-side returning ships. The abundance of vegetables it contained—from zucchini to spinach to eggplant—made it especially attractive to sailors just home from the sea. No wonder the Genoese called it 'Scignore Menestron'—*Mr.* Minestrone." —COLMAN ANDREWS

RECIPES

BRODETTO DI PESCE *(Adriatic Fish Soup)*, page 68; STRACCIATELLA *(Roman Egg-Drop Soup)*, page 71; PASTA E FAGIOLI *(Pasta and Beans)*, page 72; RIBOLLITA *(Twice-Cooked Tuscan Bread Soup)*, page 75; BRODO DI CARNE *(Italian Beef Broth)*, page 76; MINESTRONE GENOVESE *(Genoese Vegetable Soup)*, page 79; PAPPA AL POMODORO *(Tomato and Bread Soup)*, page 80.

Brodetto di Pesce

(Adriatic Fish Soup)

SERVES 8–12

WITH ALL those heads and bones available, who could make a better fish broth than a fishmonger—like Gigi Naccari (right center) of Venice, who served us this delicious soup.

1 ½ lbs. large whole
  shrimp
10 lbs. assorted heads,
  bones, and skin from
  non-oily fish (monkfish,
  rouget, fluke, grouper,
  red snapper, sea bass,
  halibut)
½ lb. mussels, debearded
½ lb. clams, scrubbed
6 black peppercorns
2 large ripe tomatoes
1 large white onion, peeled
  and halved
1 carrot, chopped
1 rib celery, chopped
3 tbsp. extra-virgin
  olive oil
3 cloves garlic, crushed
  and peeled
½ bunch Italian parsley,
  trimmed and chopped
1 cup tocai friulano or
  other dry Friuli white
  wine
Salt and freshly ground
  black pepper
1 ½ lbs. assorted filets
  from non-oily fish (as
  above), cut into 2" pieces
Freshly grated
  parmigiano-reggiano

1. Peel shrimp and pull off their heads, then put heads and shells into a large, heavy pot. Cut shrimp into large pieces and set aside in refrigerator. Add fish heads, bones, and skin, mussels, clams, peppercorns, tomatoes, onion, carrot, celery, and 4 quarts cold water to the pot, cover, and bring to a boil over high heat. Reduce heat to medium, uncover, and simmer for 1 hour, skimming foam often. Remove pot from heat, cover, and set aside for 20–30 minutes to allow any sediment to settle. Strain broth through a cheesecloth-lined strainer into a large bowl. Discard solids and rinse pot.

2. Heat oil in the same pot over medium heat. Add garlic and cook until fragrant and light brown, about 30 seconds. Remove garlic from oil and discard. Add parsley and swirl in pot for a few seconds, then add wine and cook until alcohol has evaporated, 3–5 minutes.

3. Add strained fish broth to pot, leaving any broth with sediment behind. Increase heat to medium-high and boil until broth has reduced by about one-third. You should have 10–12 cups of broth. Season to taste with salt and pepper. (Broth may be made up to this point and refrigerated or frozen until ready to be used.)

4. Bring broth to a gentle simmer over medium heat. Add pieces of fish filet and shrimp and poach until just cooked through, 2–3 minutes. Adjust seasonings. Ladle broth into bowls and sprinkle with parmigiano. Serve with toasted crusty bread brushed with a little olive oil, if you like.

Fish Stews

Fish soups and stews were originally fisherman's fare, mostly meant to use up seafood that was not easily salable on dry land; every stretch of Italian coastline had its own version. Today, such dishes have become restaurant specialties and are often based on pricey pesce—but regional differences and traditional ingredients persist. Here are some of the most popular examples of the genre:

◆ BRODETTO A term used on Italy's Adriatic coast. Some recipes call for an assortment of fish, but some use only one variety—sole in Ancona and eel in the Romagna, for example.

◆ BURIDDA A classic Ligurian fish soup, typically including several kinds of fish, as well as squid and perhaps eel. An old interpretation of buridda is made from only stockfish (dried cod) and potatoes.

◆ CACCIUCCO Literally, a "mixture" of seafood, (see page 189) originally from Livorno, on the Tuscan coast. An essential ingredient: garlic.

◆ CIUPPIN Another Ligurian dish, a fish stew in the form of a thick purée. San Francisco's cioppino borrows its name, if not its form, from this dish.

◆ ZUPPA An all-purpose term used all over Italy for almost any seafood-filled soup.

Stracciatella

(Roman Egg-Drop Soup)

SERVES 8

JANE MARIANI of Antico Ristorante Pagnanelli in Castel Gandolfo, near Rome, told us how to make this soup, so named because the eggs look like *straccetti*, or "little rags".

8 cups chicken stock
2 eggs
½ cup freshly grated
   parmigiano-reggiano
2 tbsp. minced fresh
   Italian parsley
   (optional)
Juice of half a lemon
Salt and freshly ground
   black pepper

1. Bring chicken stock to a boil in a large pot over medium-high heat, then reduce heat to medium-low. Beat eggs in a mixing bowl and add parmigiano (and parsley, if using). Slowly pour egg mixture into stock, stirring with a whisk. (The faster you stir, the finer the pieces of egg.) Season to taste with lemon juice, salt, and pepper.

Roman Holiday

Spring is the most delicious time of all in the Eternal City. As Easter—*Pasqua* in Italian—approaches, the ancient city, built on the ruins of ruins and filled with the ghosts of other ages, suddenly becomes young, fresh, virginal. It is one of Rome's paradoxes that this definitive Christian feast somehow captures the essence of the ancient capital, renewing it with timeless rites of spring. Crowds await an Easter blessing from the Pope outside Saint Peter's. Shops are done up like Fabergé eggs, with ribbons and bows framing the windows. The streets, redolent of honey-sweet flowers and roasting lamb, have a festive, pagan air. A woman sells palm fronds (right) for Palm Sunday. "Easter week has always been my favorite time of year to visit Rome," says writer David Downie, who spent several years of his childhood in the city (and who has written a book on Roman cooking, *Cucina Romana*, to be published by HarperCollins). "The season's first outdoor diners tuck into pyramids of fried zucchini blossoms stuffed with mozzarella and anchovies, mounds of fresh fava beans to be popped from their skins and eaten raw, butter-soft artichokes marinated in olive oil, and, most of all, platters of abbacchio, the suckling lamb that defines the Roman springtime table. Cool frascati wine, meanwhile, flows like the Fontana di Trevi, and all is well in the Eternal City. And for Romans, Easter feasting doesn't end on Easter Sunday. Easter Monday, called *Pasquetta* [Little Easter], is a lighthearted day for country picnics—for *una scampagnata fuori porta*, an excursion beyond the old city gates."

Pod People

The Italians love beans—both the legumes of the Old World, like chickpeas, favas, and lentils, and such New World–derived varieties as borlotti and cannellini. Some beans (e.g., the toscanelli, sorane, and zolfini so prized by the Tuscans—who are probably Italy's greatest bean eaters, incidentally) are primarily consumed locally. Here are the five most popular all over Italy; all are used dried and fresh (in season):

• BORLOTTI Cultivated mostly in the north, these speckled red-and-white beans are similar to America's cranberry beans.

• CANNELLINI These medium-size white beans (below), originally from Tuscany, are widely available both canned and dried.

• CECI, or chickpeas, are a southern favorite, usually cooked with pasta or in soups and stews.

• FAVA BEANS, a year-round staple in Puglia, were once consumed raw—pods and all—by Romans.

• LENTICCHIE, or brown lentils, believed to be one of the world's oldest cultivated foods, are traditionally eaten in Italy on New Year's Day for good luck.

Pasta e Fagioli
(Pasta and Beans)

SERVES 6

OUR FRIEND Gigi Naccari says of this dish, "Everyone uses the same basic ingredients, but some make a masterpiece, others make nothing. You must make it with *heart*."

12 oz. dried borlotti or cranberry beans, soaked overnight
2 oz. pancetta, minced
1½ cups extra-virgin olive oil
1 large yellow onion, peeled and minced
½ rib celery, trimmed and minced
3 sprigs fresh Italian parsley, trimmed and minced
2 tbsp. tomato paste
3 cloves garlic, crushed and peeled
2 small sprigs fresh rosemary
3 fresh sage leaves
Salt and freshly ground black pepper
6 oz. fettuccine, broken into small pieces

1. Drain beans and put into a large, heavy pot. Add pancetta, 1 cup of the oil, onions, celery, parsley, tomato paste, and 6½ cups cold water. Mince 1 clove of the garlic and leaves from 1 sprig of rosemary and add to pot. Bring to a boil over high heat, then reduce heat to medium-low and simmer, stirring occasionally, until beans are very tender, about 2½ hours.

2. Meanwhile, heat remaining ½ cup oil in a medium skillet over medium heat. Add sage, remaining 2 cloves garlic, and 1 sprig rosemary and cook until garlic is golden, about 3 minutes. Remove and discard sage, garlic, and rosemary from oil. Reserve flavored oil.

3. Transfer half the beans and cooking liquid to the bowl of a food processor fitted with a metal blade and purée until smooth. Stir back into pot, then stir in flavored oil and season to taste with salt and pepper.

4. Add pasta to soup and cook, stirring often, until tender, about 15 minutes. Garnish with parsley and a drizzle of olive oil, if you like.

Ribollita

(Twice-Cooked Tuscan Bread Soup)

SERVES 12

THIS FAMOUS soup is a fixture on every Tuscan trattoria menu. Although it's traditionally made a day or more before serving and then reheated, it may also be eaten fresh.

1 lb. dried cannellini
  beans
½ cup plus 2 tbsp. fruity
  extra-virgin olive oil
2 cloves garlic, crushed
4–5 fresh sage leaves
Salt and freshly ground
  black pepper
2 medium yellow onions,
  peeled and chopped
2 carrots, peeled and
  thickly sliced
2 ribs celery, trimmed and
  thickly sliced
2 medium potatoes, peeled
  and thickly sliced
1 large bunch swiss chard,
  trimmed and coarsely
  chopped
1 bunch cavolo nero or
  kale, trimmed and
  coarsely chopped
½ small savoy cabbage,
  cored and coarsely
  chopped
1 cup chopped canned
  Italian plum tomatoes
3 thick slices day-old
  country white bread

1. Cover beans with cold water and soak in a large pot for at least 4 hours or overnight. Drain, then add 12 cups water, 2 tbsp. of the oil, garlic, and sage. Cover and bring to a simmer over medium heat. Season to taste with salt, reduce heat to medium-low, and gently simmer, stirring occasionally with a wooden spoon, until beans are tender, 1–2 hours more. Season to taste with salt and pepper.

2. Remove beans from heat, set aside, and allow beans to cool in cooking liquid. Reserve 1 cup cooked beans, then purée remaining beans along with the cooking liquid and set aside.

3. Heat ¼ cup of the oil in the same casserole over medium-low heat. Add onions and cook until soft, about 20 minutes. Add carrots, celery, potatoes, chard, cavolo nero, and cabbage, stirring well. Add tomatoes, cover, and cook until greens wilt, about 20 minutes.

4. Add puréed beans and simmer, covered, for about 1 hour. Add bread and reserved beans, stir gently, cover, return to a simmer, and cook about 10 minutes more. Season to taste with salt and pepper, then refrigerate overnight.

5. The next day, preheat oven to 375°. Heat soup in a casserole in the oven, uncovered, stirring occasionally for about 30 minutes, then cook for 30 minutes more without stirring. Drizzle with remaining ¼ cup oil and serve.

Cooking Beans

C ooking beans correctly is a matter taken very seriously in Tuscany. Marco Noferi, a farmer in Paterna, not far from Arezzo, explained to writer Lori Zimring de Mori the three cardinal components for preparing dried beans so that they end up tender but firm, with a dense, rich flavor: time (cook them for at least two hours, more if the beans are old), temperature (use the lowest possible heat, so that the water barely simmers—"Boiling them in a metal pot kills half the flavor," adds Noferi), and olive oil (use the very best and freshest available). "You can't really talk about beans without talking about olive oil," Noferi maintains.

Brodo di Carne

(Italian Beef Broth)

SERVES 6

ITALIAN BROTHS, the basis for soups and some sauces, are made with meat, meaty bones, and/or pieces of fowl— unlike France's stocks, based on bones and meat scraps.

1 rib celery, trimmed
   and cut into 3 pieces
1 medium carrot, peeled,
   trimmed, and cut into
   3 pieces
1 medium white onion,
   peeled
1 large chicken leg and
   thigh
4 lbs. beef shank bones,
   with meat and marrow
1 3-oz. piece parmigiano-
   reggiano rind, with
   waxy outside layer
   scraped off with a knife
3 tbsp. salt

1. Put celery, carrot, onion, chicken, beef bones, and parmigiano rind into a large stockpot. Cover with 4 quarts cold water. Bring to a boil over high heat, skimming any foam or fat that comes to the surface. When foam rises more slowly to surface, add salt, cover, and reduce heat to low. Simmer, checking and skimming occasionally, for about 2½ hours.

2. Taste broth and adjust salt if necessary. Strain broth through a fine-mesh strainer or a cheesecloth-lined colander into a large bowl. Discard solids. When broth has cooled to room temperature, cover and refrigerate or freeze for up to 6 months.

Sisters in the Kitchen

Like all good Italian women of earlier generations, twin sisters Margherita and Valeria Simili (facing page, from left) grew up in the kitchen—but in their case, there was more to it than that. Their father, Armando, was Bologna's best-loved baker, and by the time they turned 12 they were working behind the counter and in the back of his shop, making breads and pastas. In the mid-1970s, while Marcella and Victor Hazan were researching Marcella's *The Classic Italian Cook Book*, the tome that launched her career, they sought out the Simili bakery— where they immediately clicked with the sisters. When the Hazans started a cooking school in Bologna a few years later, they hired the Similis. In 1989, with the Hazans' help, the sisters, having discovered a passion for cooking of all kinds (not just baking), opened a little cooking school of their own— where they have taught us how to make some of the cornerstones of Italian cooking, from brodo to bolognese sauce (see page 125) to lasagne (see page 126).

Minestrone Genovese

(Genoese Vegetable Soup)

SERVES 6–8

YOU MAY substitute or add cauliflower, turnips, carrots, and/or other fresh vegetables to the ingredients called for below—but don't use stock; the vegetables make their own.

1 oz. dried porcini
¼ lb. swiss chard, stems removed
¼ lb. spinach, stems removed
Salt
2 small zucchini, diced
2 medium white potatoes, peeled and diced
2 Japanese eggplants, peeled and diced
2 tbsp. extra-virgin olive oil
2 cups tubetti pasta
2 cups cooked white beans (see page 75, step 1)
2 tbsp. pesto (see page 86, step 1)
Freshly ground black pepper

1. Soak porcini in 2 cups warm water until soft, about 20 minutes. Remove porcini, rinse, chop, and set aside. Pour porcini water through a coffee filter and reserve. Chop chard and spinach leaves.

2. Bring porcini water and 6 cups salted water to a boil in a large pot. Add porcini, chard, spinach, zucchini, potatoes, eggplant, and oil. Reduce heat to low and simmer, uncovered, for 1 hour.

3. Add pasta to soup. Cook pasta for about 10 minutes, add beans, and cook 5 minutes longer. Stir in pesto and season with salt and pepper. Serve hot or, in the Genoese tradition, at room temperature. Sprinkle with grated parmigiano-reggiano, if you like.

No Meat, Please, We're Genoese

Vegetable soup in one form or another is eaten all over Italy, but the two most famous minestrones are the Milanese and Genoese interpretations. Although both include a host of seasonal vegetables, and although they can be quite similar today, there have traditionally been some distinctions between the two: the Milanese added onions, for instance, while the Genoese did not; the Milanese were more likely to add protein in the form of pancetta and/or lardo (which is more or less Italian bacon), while the Genoese used at most a bit of anchovy; the Milanese often added rice to their minestrone, while the Genoese preferred short noodles of some kind. Oh, and in Genoa, the minestrone was (and still is) always finished with a spoonful or two of the city's emblematic sauce—pesto.

Italy's Favorite Herb

I f you're Italian, it is second nature to
have a basil plant perched on your
kitchen windowsill—or, at the very
least, a few basil sprigs with roots intact in a
glass of water on a countertop. Having
reached Italy by way of Africa and India, this
aromatic herb is now available everywhere
in the country, all year long—although its name,
basilico in Italian, derives from the Greek
basilikon, meaning "regal", perhaps suggesting
that it was once a rarity. There are four main
basil varieties in Italy: genovese, the most
famous type, an essential ingredient of pesto
(see page 86); napoletano, which has shorter
leaves and a more delicate flavor; fine (thin),
which has small leaves; and mammouth, with
large leaves suitable for drying. Experts
suggest that if you have fresh basil, of whatever
type, at your disposal, you gather the leaves
slightly before the plant flowers (while more
essential oils are present), and in the early
afternoon (after the leaves have been exposed
to the sun, releasing aroma). Connoisseurs
also counsel that you should always tear basil
into pieces by hand, never chop it with a knife;
when basil comes into contact with metal, they
say, its flavor changes, and not for the better.

Pappa al Pomodoro

(Tomato and Bread Soup)

SERVES 6

LIKE RIBOLLITA, this homey dish is made with day-
old bread. Although this tomato and bread soup can be found
throughout Italy, the Florentine version is the most regal.

6 *lbs. large ripe tomatoes*
1 *cup extra-virgin
    olive oil*
5 *cloves garlic, peeled
    and chopped*
*Leaves from 1 small
    bunch basil, washed,
    with larger leaves torn
    in half*
*Salt and freshly ground
    black pepper*
2 *1-lb. loaves day-old
    Italian country-style
    bread (or any chewy,
    coarse-crumb bread),
    crusts removed*

1. Core and stem tomatoes and make a small cross incision on the bottom of each, then plunge them into a large
pot of boiling water for about 1 minute to loosen skins.
Remove tomatoes from pot with a slotted spoon and
transfer them to a large bowl of ice water. Peel tomatoes,
discarding skins, then cut them in half crosswise. Squeeze
out and discard seeds and set tomato halves aside.

2. Heat ½ cup of the oil in a large, heavy pot over
medium-high heat. Add garlic and sauté, stirring
with a wooden spoon, until soft but not brown, about
2 minutes. Add tomato halves and basil (reserving
some for garnish) and season generously with salt and
pepper. Reduce heat to medium and simmer, stirring
occasionally, until tomatoes begin to fall apart and
turn saucelike, about 30 minutes.

3. Tear bread into chunks and add to same pot with
just enough water to cover the bread, 4–5 cups. Stir to
mix well and to be sure that tomatoes don't stick to
bottom of pot. Add remaining ½ cup of oil, then
adjust seasoning if necessary. Simmer over medium
heat, stirring occasionally, until bread and tomatoes
fall apart (break up any large chunks with the back of
a wooden spoon) and soup becomes thick and silky.
Serve garnished with reserved basil leaves and drizzle
with more olive oil, if you like.

PASTA,

RISOTTO, AND POLENTA

"ONE day, in the hills above Recco, I

watched Maria Pozzo Benvenuto making

trofie—Ligurian gnocchi—on an old flour-

dusted board, mixing flour and hot water

into dough, shaping it, then pinching off

small bits and rolling them up, then back,

into perfect little corkscrews." —COLMAN ANDREWS

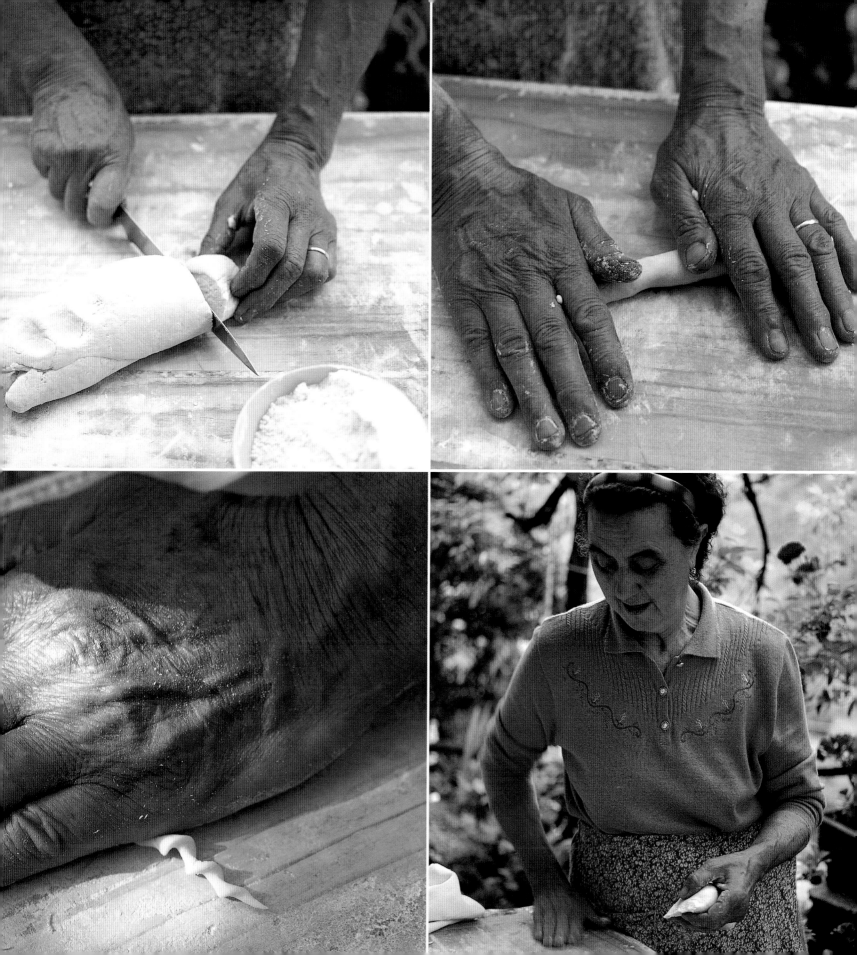

Mortar and Pesto

The first time I tasted pesto," says SAVEUR kitchen director Melissa Hamilton, "I thought that I'd never had anything so delicious in all my life. The silky texture and powerful flavors of basil, pine nuts, garlic, olive oil, and parmigiano crushed together with a mortar and pestle were so perfectly balanced, I could have eaten the pesto by the spoonful—to hell with the pasta. After a few years of making big batches of pesto in my blender, however—and finding it on everything from chicken to pizza when I went out to eat—it lost its charm. For years, in fact, I found that I could barely look at the stuff, let alone eat it. Then it dawned on me: the thing that separates a boring pesto from a sublime one (besides the obvious—unblemished basil leaves with no stems, good oil, nuts that aren't rancid) is the tool with which it's made. Pesto from a blender can be sharp and unbalanced. The right tool, of course, is the traditional mortar and pestle, which gently crushes and blends the pungent flavors. Our favorite version of this ancient machinery [above] is heavy, with a slightly rough texture inside—the kind that pharmacists used to use. Truth is, crushing all that basil into a paste may seem daunting at first, but it's great fun once you get into the rhythm."

Trofie al Pesto
(Ligurian Gnocchi with Pesto)

SERVES 6

RECCO, which might be called the culinary capital of eastern Liguria, is known for this pasta. Handmade trofie are best, but acceptable commercial trofie are also available.

FOR PESTO:
2 tightly packed cups
  stemless fresh basil
  leaves
2 tbsp. pine nuts
2 cloves garlic, peeled
  and chopped
Coarse salt
½ cup mild extra-virgin
  olive oil
½ cup grated parmigiano-
  reggiano

FOR TROFIE:
3 cups flour, plus extra to
  work with
1 tsp. salt

½ lb. haricots verts
  or small string beans,
  trimmed and cut into
  2" pieces
5 new potatoes, peeled

1. For pesto, crush basil, pine nuts, garlic, and a large pinch of salt into a fine paste with a mortar and pestle. Drizzle in oil, stirring constantly, then stir in parmigiano. Put plastic wrap directly on surface of pesto, then set aside. If using a food processor, put pine nuts, garlic, and salt into the bowl of the processor fitted with a metal blade and blend to a paste. Add basil, drizzle in oil, and process until smooth. Transfer to a bowl and stir in parmigiano.

2. For trofie, sift flour and salt together into a mound on a clean surface. Use your hand to make a well in the center, then pour in about 1¼ cups water. Flour your hands, then knead flour and water together with both hands until dough is soft and no longer sticky. Push dough to one side, clean surface and hands, then flour both again and knead dough again, adding more flour if necessary, until it is very smooth, 2–3 minutes. Cover dough with a kitchen towel and set aside for half an hour.

3. Clean and flour hands and surface again. Pinch off a pea-size piece of dough and roll it away from you with the palm of your hand to form a fat matchstick. Turn your hand up at a 45° angle, then gently roll the matchstick back toward you to form a spiral shape with two pointed ends (see page 85, bottom left). Repeat to use all the dough. This may take practice; expect to throw away some ill-formed trofie at first. As trofie are made, transfer to a lightly floured parchment-lined baking sheet.

4. Cook haricots in a pot of boiling salted water over high heat until tender, about 5 minutes. Remove haricots with a slotted spoon, then add potatoes to the same water and boil until soft, about 15 minutes. Remove potatoes with a slotted spoon, allow to cool, then slice thinly. Cook trofie in the same water over high heat until they float to the surface, about 4 minutes. Dilute pesto with 2 tbsp. of pasta water, then drain pasta, transfer to a large bowl, and mix with pesto, potatoes, and haricots.

Mandilli de Sæa al Pesto

("Silk Handkerchiefs" with Pesto)

SERVES 6–8

THE DELICATE pasta sheets called mandilli de sæa ("silk handkerchiefs" in Genoese) are one of the rare Ligurian pastas made with eggs. This recipe is from Gianni Belforte of the Circolo Artistico Tunnel, Genoa's oldest private club.

3 cups flour
½ tsp. salt
5 eggs
3 tbsp. extra-virgin
    olive oil
1 recipe pesto (see page 86,
    step 1)
Freshly grated
    parmigiano-reggiano

1. Sift flour and salt together into a mound on a clean surface. Use your hand to make a well in the center, then break eggs into the well. Lightly beat eggs with a fork, then gradually incorporate flour from the inside edge of the well into eggs. When dough becomes too stiff to work with the fork, knead flour into eggs with both hands until dough is no longer sticky; form dough into a ball and wrap in plastic. Clean your board and hands.

2. Unwrap dough and knead with the heel of your hand until dough is smooth, about 5 minutes. Cut dough into 5 equal pieces and flatten it so it will fit through the rollers of a hand-cranked pasta machine. Set rollers of pasta machine at widest setting, then feed pasta through rollers 3 or 4 times, folding and turning pasta until it is smooth and the width of the machine.

3. Roll pasta through machine again through each setting to the finest notch, decreasing the settings one notch at a time (do not fold or turn pasta). Keep each pasta sheet and unrolled dough covered with damp towels. When pasta sheets are done, cut each one into about 12 4" squares. Set squares aside, layered between wax paper.

4. Bring a large pot of salted water to a boil over high heat. Add 1 tbsp. oil and half the pasta and cook until pasta is tender, 3–4 minutes. Remove carefully with a slotted spoon, drain in a colander, and toss with 1 tbsp. of the oil. Repeat process with remaining pasta. Dilute pesto with ½ cup of pasta-cooking water. Gently toss hot pasta with pesto and serve with parmigiano.

Alternative Pesto

The term *pesto* has been appropriated in recent years by creative young chefs and food marketers, to describe culinary pastes of many kinds. Thus we encounter cilantro–green chile pesto, sun-dried-tomato pesto, Asian pesto, Caribbean pesto, and who knows what else. These inventions may indeed be taking the idea of pesto a bit far afield, but it is worth noting that not all authentic pesto has always been made with basil. The Genoese poet and playwright Vito Elio Petrucci, a founding member of the Confraternità del Pesto, or Pesto Brotherhood, has reported that when summer basil disappeared for the season every year and greenhouse basil began appearing in the markets at a higher price, his mother would exclaim of the merchants who were selling it, "Son' furti, son' laddri!"—"They're thieves, they're robbers!"—and promptly start making her pesto with parsley instead until prices dropped again. Before the advent of greenhouse basil in the late 1920s, other non-basil pestos were sometimes made in Liguria, especially in rural regions. It was simply a matter of adapting to the season. Not only parsley but marjoram, arugula, and even baby swiss chard leaves were used—although probably not cilantro or green chiles.

Arrivederci Romas

I 've discovered," reports journalist Robert Ragaini, "that the words 'San Marzano' on an imported can of Italian plum tomatoes may refer to San Marzano the town, not to san marzano the tomato variety, and that the can could therefore just as easily contain roma tomatoes, which are also grown and canned in the San Marzano region but are quite different in taste. I found out how different in San Marzano itself, at the Punto Verde canning plant. Several newly washed romas were lying next to some just-picked san marzanos. The san marzanos were thin and pointed (*scrawny* would be a most appropriate word), while the romas were plump and glowing with health. I tried a roma first and found it mild, juicy, and very pleasant, albeit a bit bland. In contrast, the san marzano was meatier and drier, with a much stronger, much better taste. 'It's not like candy or cake,' said my interpreter proudly. 'In the san marzano tomato, less is more!'" New Yorker Nick Soccodato imports canned san marzano tomatoes into the United States. His wife, Rose, uses them for her classic tomato sauce (right), an Italian basic that can be used in many recipes.

Spaghetti al Pomodoro
(*Spaghetti with Tomato Sauce*)

SERVES 4

TASTING pasta throughout Italy has given us a new understanding of the term *al dente*; it doesn't just mean firm—it implies a real, if slight, resistance to the tooth. When Italians cook dried pasta, they like it to be almost underdone by American standards; the wheatiness of the pasta becomes an important part of the flavor experience.

3 tbsp. extra-virgin olive oil
2 cloves garlic, peeled and chopped
1 28-oz. can peeled whole san marzano tomatoes
Salt and freshly ground black pepper
3 fresh basil leaves, minced
1 lb. spaghetti
Freshly grated parmigiano-reggiano

1. Heat oil in a earthenware or enameled cast-iron pot over medium heat. Add garlic and sauté, stirring frequently, until golden, about 3 minutes. Add tomatoes, along with the juice from the can. Season to taste with salt and pepper.

2. Increase heat to high, bring sauce to a boil, and cook until liquid has reduced slightly, about 5 minutes. Reduce heat to medium-low and simmer, stirring occasionally, for about 30 minutes. Add basil leaves and cook for 15 minutes more.

3. Meanwhile, cook spaghetti in a large pot of boiling salted water until al dente, 10–12 minutes. Drain in a colander, add pasta to sauce, and stir well. Serve with parmigiano.

Spaghetti alla Puttanesca

("Whore's Style" Spaghetti)

SERVES 4

THIS ROBUST dish, which originated on the island of Ischia in the Bay of Naples but has since become associated with Roman cooking, is said to owe its name not only to its spiciness but to the fact that it's fast and easy.

¼ cup extra-virgin
   olive oil
2 cloves garlic, peeled and
   minced
4 anchovy filets, minced
1 28-oz. can whole
   Italian plum tomatoes,
   drained and roughly
   chopped
1 cup pitted mixed green
   and black olives
2 tbsp. capers, rinsed
½ tsp. red pepper flakes
Salt
1 lb. spaghetti
Freshly grated
   parmigiano-reggiano

1. Heat oil in a large skillet over medium-high heat. Add garlic and anchovies and sauté for 20 seconds. Add tomatoes, olives, capers, and red pepper flakes and season to taste with salt. Continue to cook, stirring occasionally, for 5 minutes more. Cover and remove from heat.

2. Meanwhile, cook spaghetti in a large pot of boiling salted water until al dente, 10–12 minutes. Drain in a colander, then add to sauce, tossing until well mixed. Serve with parmigiano.

Fruit of the Land

More than 50 varieties of olives are cultivated in Italy, both for table use—as snacks or part of an antipasto selection and in cooking—and for oil. As elsewhere in the olive-eating world (in Spain and Greece, for instance), olives are cured in their own oil but also in water or in salt and may be flavored with a host of herbs and spices. Popular table olive varieties include ascolana, cerignola, nocellara, and the Spanish-born manzanilla, although the tiny niçoise-like taggiasca, the principal oil olive in Liguria, has its champions, too. The small black olive di Gaeta is particularly popular for cooking.

Cheek or Stomach?

Pancetta (above), literally "little stomach", is lean, characteristically sweet, salt-cured pig belly—in effect, unsmoked bacon—typically rolled into a cylindrical shape and used throughout Italy to add richness and salty flavor to a wide range of dishes. Guanciale derives its name from the Italian *guancia*, or cheek, and is fatty, salt-cured pig's jowl, usually rectangular in shape. Romans insist that you can't make certain classic dishes of their region without guanciale—for instance, bucatini all'amatriciana (see page 98)—but the truth is that pancetta works perfectly well; probably only a Roman could tell the difference anyway.

Spaghetti alla Carbonara

(*Spaghetti with Eggs and Pancetta*)

SERVES 4

ROMANS SAY that this pasta was introduced to their city by the charcoal sellers who came down from Abruzzo in earlier times to hawk their wares—which is why they've named it for the *carbonara*, the charcoal maker's wife.

1 tbsp. extra-virgin
olive oil
5 oz. pancetta cut into
¼" × ¼" dice
2 eggs plus 2 egg yolks
1 lb. spaghetti
½ cup freshly grated
parmigiano-reggiano
½ cup freshly grated
pecorino romano

1. Heat oil in a skillet over medium-high heat. Add pancetta and fry until crisp and brown, 5–6 minutes.

2. Put eggs, egg yolks, and ¼ cup water into a small bowl and beat together with a fork, then set aside.

3. Cook spaghetti in a large pot of boiling salted water until al dente, 10–12 minutes. Drain in a colander, then return spaghetti to the pot. Use 2 large forks or spoons to mix the eggs, the pancetta with all its rendered fat and cooking oil, and ¼ cup each of the parmigiano and pecorino into spaghetti. Serve with the remaining ¼ cup each parmigiano and pecorino sprinkled on top.

Spaghetti all'Astice

(Spaghetti with Lobster)

SERVES 4

ATLANTIC lobster is hardly a typical Venetian ingredient, but at his popular, informal Mascaron, Gigi Vianello delights his customers with this simple but luxurious dish.

1 1–1½-lb. live Maine
   lobster
3 tbsp. extra-virgin
   olive oil
1 clove garlic, peeled and
   minced
1 cup tocai friulano or
   other dry Friuli white
   wine
4 ripe tomatoes, cored,
   seeded, and chopped
Salt
1 lb. spaghetti
4 sprigs fresh Italian
   parsley, trimmed
   and chopped

1. Plunge a sharp knife into top of lobster's head just behind its eyes (to kill it quickly), then use a large chef's knife or cleaver to chop it into 8–10 pieces.

2. Heat oil in a large skillet over medium-high heat. Add lobster with any juices and garlic and cook, stirring and turning the lobster pieces, for 1 minute. Add wine and cook until alcohol has evaporated, about 3 minutes. Add tomatoes and cook, stirring occasionally and breaking tomatoes up with the back of a wooden spoon, until sauce gets smoother and thickens slightly, about 10 minutes. Season to taste with salt.

3. Meanwhile, cook spaghetti in a large pot of boiling salted water until al dente, 10–12 minutes. Drain in a colander, add pasta to sauce, stirring well, and cook for a few minutes more. Serve garnished with parsley.

Behind the Mask

The roguishly energetic Gigi Vianello (above) sets the tone for Mascaron (the word means "large carnival mask" in Venetian dialect), his always bustling wine bar turned restaurant in the heart of Venice. (You'll probably have to share a table, but it will almost certainly be with somebody interesting.) He welcomes guests warmly, banters with them, walks them out on his arm; he talks on his cell phone and serves plates of pasta at the same time. He doesn't make a big thing out of his food—but when he offers you dishes like his stockfish puréed with olive oil, scallops in tomato sauce, or spaghetti with lobster, you'll know that, no matter how much fun Mascaron is, it's a serious restaurant.

Summer Pasta

O ne of the Lazio region's famous dishes comes not from Rome but from the nearby countryside—specifically, from Amatrice (below), a tiny mountain town in the province of Rieti, near the border between Lazio and Abruzzi. The dish is bucatini all'amatriciana (see recipe, right), and it's the centerpiece of Amatrice's Sagra degli Spaghetti, or spaghetti festival (bucatini are in effect hollow spaghetti), held each year on the first Sunday following the big Italian holiday of Ferragosto—August 15, the Feast of the Assumption. (The pasta sometimes appears on menus as "alla matriciana", but that's an error.) Locals say that their famous sauce probably originated as a shepherd's dish across the line in Abruzzo and claim an ancient heritage for it. The original, they say, predated the widespread use of tomatoes in Italy—and a tomatoless version is sometimes seen on menus in the region under the name bucatini alla gricia, after Griciano, another local town.

Bucatini all'Amatriciana
(Hollow Noodles with Amatrice-Style Tomato Sauce)

SERVES 4

THIS IS one dish for which Romans insist on using guanciale, or cured pork jowl (see page 94)—but, as noted, it's almost impossible to find in the U.S., and pancetta works fine.

3 tbsp. extra-virgin
  olive oil
6 oz. pancetta, finely diced
½ tsp. red pepper flakes
2 cups finely chopped
  tomatoes
2 tbsp. freshly grated
  parmigiano-reggiano
1 cup freshly grated
  pecorino romano
Salt
1 lb. bucatini

1. Heat oil in a large skillet over medium heat. Add pancetta and cook until crisp, about 10 minutes, then transfer with a slotted spoon to paper towels to drain, and set aside.

2. Increase heat to medium-high, carefully add red pepper flakes and tomatoes to the hot oil in the pan, and cook, stirring often, until sauce thickens slightly, 6–8 minutes. Reduce heat to medium, add parmigiano and 2 tbsp. of the pecorino, and cook for a few minutes longer.

3. Meanwhile, cook bucatini in a large pot of boiling salted water until al dente, about 10–12 minutes. Drain in a colander, then transfer pasta to skillet with sauce, add 2–3 tbsp. pecorino, and stir until well coated. Divide bucatini between 4 bowls and sprinkle each with some reserved pancetta and a bit more pecorino.

Bigoli in Salsa

(Whole Wheat Spaghetti with Anchovy Sauce)

SERVES 4

AT THEIR charming and popular Da Fiore in Venice, Maurizio and Mara Martin serve a wide choice of excellent dishes both innovative and traditional. Mara's version of this Venetian classic is the most satisfying we've found.

8 oz. whole salt-packed anchovies (about 32 fish)
1½ cups tocai friulano or other dry Friuli white wine
½ cup extra-virgin olive oil
1 large yellow onion, peeled, halved, and thinly sliced
1 lb. bigoli or whole wheat spaghetti
Salt

1. Soak anchovies in ½ cup of the white wine and 2 cups water in a large bowl for 30 minutes. Gently pull anchovies apart into lengthwise halves from the head end and remove and discard spines and all tiny bones. Rinse anchovies in the soaking liquid, then discard the liquid. Set aside 8 anchovy halves for garnish, then cut remaining halves into small pieces and set aside.

2. Heat oil in a large skillet over medium heat. Add onions and cut-up anchovies and cook, breaking up anchovies with the back of a wooden spoon, until onions are very soft and anchovies have "melted", about 10 minutes. Add remaining cup of wine and stir, scraping up any brown bits stuck to bottom of skillet. Reduce heat to low, cover, and cook for about 30 minutes, stirring occasionally.

3. Meanwhile, cook bigoli in a large pot of boiling lightly salted water (the anchovies are very salty) until al dente, 10–12 minutes. Drain in a colander, add pasta to sauce, mix well, and serve garnished with reserved anchovies and with parsley sprigs, if you like.

Regional Pasta

In addition to the standard pasta sizes and shapes found all over Italy, there are local pastas traditional to each of Italy's regions. In the Veneto the best known is probably the thick, round noodles called bigoli. The pasta gets its name from the *bigolaro*, or hand press, from which the dough is extruded, giving it its rough texture—perfect for embracing sauce. Traditional bigoli are made with farina di grano tenero (soft-grain flour), not the semola di grano duro (durum, or hard-grain, flour) of which most pastas are composed. But whole wheat bigoli, like those used at Da Fiore in Venice, are common, too.

Useful Kernels

P ine nuts, used in so many traditional Italian and other Mediterranean dishes, are not really nuts, but the seeds from pine cones. There are as many varieties of these seeds as there are varieties of pine, obviously, but two—known simply in the marketplace as Mediterranean and Asian—are used for most gastronomic purposes. While both varieties have a thin shell (removed before they're packaged for sale) with an ivory-colored nut meat, the Asian pine nut is teardrop-shaped and the Mediterranean pine nut is elongated. But the real distinction is one of flavor: Mediterranean pine nuts (above, foreground) are mild and delicate, and preferable for Italian cooking; their Asian counterparts (above, middle and rear) are slightly pungent, with a hint of pine flavor. Both kinds have a high oil content and thus can turn rancid quickly. It's a good idea to taste or smell your pine nuts before you commit them to whatever dish you're making; if they're sour, just leave them out.

Bucatini con le Sarde

(Hollow Noodles with Sardines)

SERVES 6

LEGEND HAS it that this pasta, considered Sicily's national dish, was invented by ninth-century Arab army cooks on the island, who, seeking ingredients to feed the troops, found wild fennel in the hills and fresh sardines in the harbors. Cultivated fennel and canned sardines work perfectly well.

½ cup dried currants
Salt
Green fronds of 3 fennel
  bulbs, trimmed of main
  stems (reserve bulbs for
  another use)
¾ cup extra-virgin
  olive oil
1 cup fresh bread crumbs
1 large yellow onion, peeled
  and finely chopped
6 anchovy filets
2 4-oz. cans sardines,
  drained of their oil
Freshly ground black
  pepper
½ cup pine nuts
½ tsp. saffron
1 lb. bucatini

1. Put currants into a small bowl, cover with hot water, and set aside to plump for at least 15 minutes. Fill a large pot with 3 quarts of water, add several large pinches of salt, and bring to a boil over high heat. Add fennel fronds and cook for 2 minutes. Remove fennel with a slotted spoon and set aside to let cool. Reserve fennel water to cook pasta. Coarsely chop cooled fennel.

2. Meanwhile, heat 2 tbsp. of the oil in a large, heavy skillet over medium-high heat. Add bread crumbs and cook, stirring, until golden, 2–3 minutes. Transfer to a bowl and set aside.

3. Heat ½ cup of the oil in a large saucepan over medium heat. Add onions and sauté, stirring with a wooden spoon, until soft but not browned, about 5 minutes. Add anchovies and cook for 3 minutes more. Stir sardines in gently, without breaking them up too much. Season to taste with salt and pepper. Drain currants and add, along with pine nuts and fennel greens, to saucepan, reduce heat to low, and simmer for 5 minutes. Remove from heat and set aside.

4. Bring the 3 quarts of fennel water back to a boil and stir in saffron. Add bucatini and cook until al dente, 10–12 minutes. Reserve about a cup of the cooking water, then drain pasta in a colander. Return pasta to the pot and stir in the fennel–sardine mixture, the remaining 2 tbsp. oil, and enough of the reserved cooking water (you may not use the whole cup) to make the pasta moist and saucy. Adjust seasoning and serve with reserved toasted bread crumbs sprinkled on top.

Tagliolini alle Vongole Veraci

(Tagliolini with Clams)

SERVES 4–8

AT RIVIERA, a trattoria facing the Giudecca Canal in Venice (left), this dish is made with vongole veraci (*Tapes decussatus*)—literally, "true clams"—which most Italians consider to be the most flavorful kind. In America, substitute littlenecks or small cherrystones (*Mercenaria mecenaria*).

6 *tbsp. extra-virgin olive oil*
1 *clove garlic, peeled and chopped*
½ *bunch Italian parsley, trimmed and chopped*
3½ *lbs. manila clams, scrubbed*
⅔ *cup tocai friulano or other dry Friuli white wine*
2 *tbsp. good-quality Italian or California brandy*
Salt
1 *recipe egg pasta (see page 122), cut into tagliolini, or 1 lb. fresh tagliolini*
1 *tbsp. grated parmigiano-reggiano*

1. Heat 5 tbsp. of the oil, along with the garlic and half the parsley, in a large skillet over medium-high heat for about 1 minute. Add clams, cover, and cook for 1 minute more. Add wine and brandy and cook, uncovered, until alcohol has evaporated, 2–3 minutes. Cover and continue cooking, shaking skillet several times, until clam shells open, about 3 minutes more (discard any that don't open). Uncover and allow liquid to reduce slightly.

2. Meanwhile, cook pasta in a large pot of boiling salted water until just tender, 1½–2 minutes (fresh pasta cooks much faster than dried). Drain in a colander. Add pasta to skillet with clams, reduce heat to medium-low, and mix well. Add parmigiano and remaining 1 tbsp. oil and season to taste with salt. Cook for 1 minute more. Serve garnished with remaining parsley.

Shell Game

When you order clams in Italy—whether with pasta or by themselves in some sort of broth or sauce—you will often get them in the shell. This isn't laziness; Italians just happen to love the idea of using the shells for scooping up the savory liquid the clams have been cooked in. Flavor aside, that's undoubtedly one reason for the popularity of the comparatively large, gray-yellow vongole veraci. The manila clam (*Tapes philippinarum*), a foreign interloper now found in the lagoon of Venice and other Mediterranean waters, is smaller and, some say, sweeter—but of not much use as a scoop. Size aside, how can you tell vongole veraci when you see them? They have a pair of horn-shaped blowholes, through which they keep themselves flushed out.

Pasta Sizes

Italians eat pasta daily—often twice a day—and have hundreds of shapes and sizes to choose from. The most popular of these in the northern reaches of the country tend to be noodles instead of little tubes or "bow ties" or other shapes. Here are some of the most common pasta strands:

- CAPELLINI (fine hairs; also called capelli d'angeli [angel's hair] or fedelini [little faithful ones]): A dry, rounded pasta about 1/16" thick.
- SPAGHETTI (little strings): Perhaps still the most widely used in everyday cooking around Italy, this dry, rounded pasta measures 1/8" thick; so does vermicelli (little worms). Spaghettoni, or vermicelloni, are slightly thicker, while spaghettini are slightly thinner.
- LINGUINE (little tongues; similar to tagliolini [little cut pieces]): A long, flat, dry pasta cut about 1/8" wide.
- FETTUCCINE (small ribbons; similar to tagliatelle [little cut pieces]): A long, flat pasta about 1/4" in width, fresh or dry.
- PAPPARDELLE (from the verb *pappare*, meaning to gobble up) Fresh or dry, this pasta measures about 1" wide.

Tagliatelle al Prosciutto
(Tagliatelle with Prosciutto)

SERVES 6

BOLOGNA'S classic meat sauce, ragù alla bolognese (see page 125), may be world famous, but this other local pasta sauce remains largely unknown outside the city itself.

¾ lb. prosciutto, cut into
　½" dice
1 cup milk
2 cups brodo di carne
　(see page 76) or chicken
　stock
1 28-oz. can whole
　Italian plum tomatoes,
　drained and puréed
Freshly ground pepper
1 recipe egg pasta (see
　page 122), cut into
　tagliatelle, or 1 lb.
　fresh tagliatelle
Salt
1 tbsp. butter, room
　temperature
½ cup freshly grated
　parmigiano-reggiano

1. Put prosciutto into a medium saucepan and cook over low heat, stirring often, until fat is translucent, about 5 minutes. Heat milk in a small pot over medium heat. Heat the broth and tomatoes together in another medium pot over medium heat.

2. Season prosciutto with freshly ground pepper and increase heat to medium-high. Add hot milk and cook, stirring with a wooden spoon, until all the milk has evaporated, 10–15 minutes. (The sauce will curdle if the milk is not "cooked out".) Add tomato–broth mixture, reduce heat to medium-low, and slowly simmer for 15 minutes, stirring occasionally.

3. Meanwhile, cook tagliatelle in a large pot of boiling salted water until just tender and pasta floats to the surface, about 30 seconds (fresh pasta cooks much faster than dried). Drain in a colander, transfer to a large, warm serving bowl, and toss with butter and parmigiano. Add prosciutto sauce and toss gently to mix well.

Pappardelle al Tartufo Nero di Norcia

(Wide Noodles with Norcia Black Truffles)

SERVES 6–8

ALTHOUGH MOST of the food at Il Fico Vecchio, outside Rome, is local, this pasta dish combines a broad Tuscan cousin of fettuccine with truffles from Norcia in Umbria.

1 oz. norcia or other fresh black truffle
12 tbsp. butter
Salt
1 recipe egg pasta (see page 122) cut into pappardelle, or 1 lb. fresh pappardelle
½ cup freshly grated parmigiano-reggiano
Freshly ground black pepper

1. Gently loosen and remove dirt from truffle with a soft mushroom brush, pick any remaining dirt out of the crevices with the tip of a paring knife, and brush again.

2. Melt butter in a large saucepan set over a pan of simmering water over medium-low heat. Finely grate two-thirds of the truffle into the melted butter and set the remaining one-third aside.

3. Cook pasta in a large pot of boiling salted water, stirring frequently, until just tender and pasta floats to the surface, 2–3 minutes (fresh pasta cooks much faster than dried). Drain in a colander, then add to saucepan with truffle butter; add ¼ cup of the parmigiano. Season to taste with salt and pepper and mix well. Allow pasta to rest briefly before serving. Shave remaining truffle over pasta and sprinkle with more parmigiano.

Delicious Fortune

Named after the Etruscan god of good fortune, Norsia, the Umbrian town of Norcia has proven to be particularly fortunate in a gastronomic sense. Although the town, founded in the second century B.C. by the Sabines, remains a small municipality, it is famous throughout Italy for four things: its pecorino cheese, its home-cured pork products (so well regarded that sausage shops are sometimes called *norcinerie*, even in other parts of Italy), its lentils, and, perhaps most of all, its black truffles. These are *Tuber melanosporum*, just like the black truffles found in France; connoisseurs may argue whether they're as good as their French cousins, but they are undeniably earthy and nutty and haunting in flavor, and they can transform a simple pasta dish into something ethereal.

Rigatoni alla Disgraziata

(Rigatoni with Eggplant and Bread Crumbs)

SERVES 6

THE NAME of this classic Sicilian pasta—the poor wretch's rigatoni—may derive from the fact that bread crumbs were a substitute for grated cheese in poor rural households.

2 medium eggplants,
 trimmed and cut into
 1" cubes
Kosher salt
1 cup plus 2 tbsp. extra-
 virgin olive oil
1 cup fresh bread crumbs
1 lb. rigatoni
¼ tsp. red pepper flakes
2 cups tomato sauce
 (see page 90, steps
 1 and 2)
¼ cup grated ricotta
 salata
Freshly grated
 parmigiano-reggiano

1. Put eggplant into a colander, sprinkle with about 3 tbsp. salt, and toss to coat well. Allow to drain for 1 hour to extract water and any bitterness. Rinse eggplant and pat dry with paper towels.

2. Meanwhile, heat 2 tbsp. of the oil in a large, heavy skillet over medium-high heat. Add bread crumbs and cook, stirring, until golden, 2–3 minutes. Transfer to a bowl and set aside.

3. Wipe out skillet, add remaining 1 cup oil, and heat over medium-high heat. Add half the eggplant and cook, stirring often, until golden, 8–10 minutes. Transfer eggplant with a slotted spoon to a large bowl and season to taste with salt. Repeat process with remaining eggplant.

4. Cook pasta in a large pot of boiling salted water until al dente, 12–15 minutes. Add red pepper flakes to red sauce in a small pot and warm over medium heat, 4–5 minutes. Drain pasta in a colander and add to bowl with eggplant. Add tomato sauce, ricotta, and bread crumbs and toss well. Serve sprinkled with parmigiano.

The Name Game

In naming dishes, the Italians often give credit where credit is due, appending the name of a city (risotto alla milanese; see page 145) or a profession. In the case of the profession, the feminine form is almost always used—since it was understood in traditional Italian life that the wife of the professional would be cooking while her husband provided the materials or the inspiration for the dish in question. In various places in this book, the carbonara, the cacciatora, the vaccinara, and the pizzaiola all get culinary credit (the name puttanesca is a slightly different case, referring to a profession in itself). Here are some other examples:

◆ ALLA CARRETTIERA (trucker's wife): A hearty, strength-providing pasta sauce made of onions, garlic, anchovies, and capers.

◆ ALLA CAVALEGGERA (cavalryman's wife): A rich pasta sauce made with walnuts, cream, parmigiano-reggiano, and eggs.

◆ ALL'ARGENTIERA (silversmith's wife): Anything garnished with fried caciocavallo cheese.

◆ ALLA GHIOTTA (glutton's wife): A sauce made from pan drippings; usually served with fish.

◆ ALLA GIARDINIERA (gardener's wife): Any dish made with fresh vegetables.

Orecchiette with Broccoli Rabe

SERVES 6

AT RAO'S, this southern Italian–style pasta is usually made with sausage added—but we had it meatless one night and liked the appealingly bitter simplicity of this version.

2 lbs. broccoli rabe, stems removed
Salt
1 lb. orecchiette
½ cup extra-virgin olive oil
7 cloves garlic, peeled and minced
Freshly ground black pepper
Freshly grated pecorino romano

1. Place broccoli rabe in a deep saucepan and cover with cold salted water. Bring to a simmer over high heat. When bubbles appear, remove from heat. Drain, plunge broccoli rabe into ice water, drain again, pat dry, and set aside.

2. Cook orecchiette in a large pot of boiling salted water until al dente, 10–12 minutes.

3. Meanwhile, heat oil in a large sauté pan over medium heat and sauté garlic until fragrant and just golden, about 3 minutes. Add broccoli rabe, season to taste with salt and pepper, and cook until warmed through, about 5 minutes. Reduce heat to low and keep warm until pasta is ready.

4. Drain pasta in a colander, then add to broccoli rabe, and toss to mix well. Remove from heat, transfer to a platter, and serve with pecorino.

Frankie No

Rao's is one of New York's last legendary Italian neighborhood joints, but making this recipe might be as close as you'll ever come to eating there. Well, *maybe* you could eat there, if you knew the right people. Otherwise, as proprietor Frank Pellegrino (far left, top) probably says into the phone a hundred times a day, "No". There just isn't room. The regulars all have regular tables, and the tables number only ten. Rao's has stood at the corner of Pleasant Avenue and 114th Street in East Harlem since 1896, when Charles Rao and his wife, Francesca, known as "Mama Jake", bought a corner saloon and named it for their family—immigrants from Polla, southeast of Naples. "The food we serve at Rao's," Pellegrino—who is known as "Frankie No", for obvious reasons—told writer Tom McNamee, "is what everybody in the neighborhood grew up eating. It's not restaurant food, it's just *cucina casalinga*—home cooking."

Friuli Tradition

For more than three-quarters of a century," writer Eugenia Bone reports, "the woodstove at Al Copari has been cooking the same traditional dishes—simple things like gnocchi, risotto, minestrone, roasted guinea hen, and frittate. Located just across a cornfield from the Slovenian border in far eastern Friuli, the farm became a hospital during World War I and was later used as a school. For many years, it had the only telephone in the area, which it made available for public use. Al Copari's proprietor today is Anna Maria Lesizza [right]. At once bawdy and ladylike, she pointedly kept her knees together when we were photographing her, telling us that the reason she wasn't rich was that 'the higher you raise your legs, the more money you earn!'"

Gnocs di Côce Zale cu Ragù

(Squash Gnocchi with Meat Sauce)

SERVES 4–6

AT AL COPARI, her trattoria in Craoretto, Anna Maria Lesizza cooks the meat and tomatoes for her ragù separately, so that the fat from the meat doesn't end up in the sauce.

FOR SAUCE:
½ lb. ground beef
½ lb. ground pork
2 tbsp. extra-virgin olive oil
Salt and freshly ground black pepper
1 large yellow onion, peeled and finely chopped
1 28-oz. can peeled whole Italian plum tomatoes, chopped

FOR GNOCCHI:
1 small butternut squash, quartered lengthwise and seeded
2 eggs
Salt
1 cup flour

1. For sauce, brown beef and pork in 1 tbsp. of the oil in a medium skillet over medium heat, using the back of a wooden spoon to break up meat. Season to taste with salt and pepper. Meanwhile, cook onions in remaining 1 tbsp. oil in another medium skillet over medium heat until soft and golden, about 20 minutes, then stir in tomatoes and their juices. Reduce heat to low and simmer, uncovered, stirring occasionally, until sauce thickens. Drain fat from meat, then add meat to tomato sauce. Adjust seasoning, then set aside.

2. For gnocchi, preheat oven to 350°. Put squash in a baking pan, cover with foil, and bake until soft, about 1 hour. Remove from oven and, when cool enough to handle, scoop out the flesh into a strainer, then press out as much liquid as you can. Transfer to a large bowl, add eggs, and mash together with a potato masher. Season to taste with salt, then work in flour to form a thick, soft dough.

3. Bring a large pot of salted water to a gentle boil over medium-high heat. Using 2 tablespoons, one to scoop up batter, the other to push each gnocchi off spoon, drop spoonfuls of batter into water. (If gnocchi fall apart, skim pieces out of water, add a little flour to batter, and try again.) Cook until gnocchi have risen to surface and simmered for 1–2 minutes. Transfer with a slotted spoon to a warm platter. Continue until all batter has been used. Spoon warm sauce over gnocchi.

Gnocchi Verdi

(Spinach Gnocchi)

SERVES 6

THIS RECIPE calls for tomato sauce, but spinach gnocchi may also be served with ragù (see page 125), simply tossed with butter and sage, or even served in brodo (see page 76).

Salt
2 large bunches spinach, trimmed
2 medium russet potatoes
½ cup flour
2 cups tomato sauce (see page 90, steps 1 and 2), finely puréed

1. Heat ¼ cup water seasoned with 1 tbsp. salt in a large pot. Add spinach leaves and cook until completely soft and wilted, about 3 minutes. Drain in a colander and, when cool enough to handle, squeeze out water. Finely chop spinach, then grind into a purée with a mortar and pestle, and set aside.

2. Put potatoes into a medium pot, cover with cold water, season with salt, and cook over medium-high heat until easily pierced with a knife, about 45 minutes. Drain in a colander. Peel potatoes while still hot, then press potatoes through a potato ricer into a mound on a lightly floured surface. Sprinkle potatoes with 2 tsp. salt, then allow potatoes to cool enough to handle.

3. Make a well in the center of potatoes, put spinach in the center, and sprinkle with ½ cup of flour. Knead and fold mixture with the heels of your hands, pushing lightly against the board, and, using a pastry scraper, lift any dough sticking to the board, until it comes together to form a smooth dough, 1–2 minutes. Add 3–4 tbsp. more flour if your dough is too soft or sticky. Do not overwork dough, or gnocchi will become tough. Set dough aside, clean surface of scraps of dough, then lightly flour. Wash, dry, and lightly flour your hands before rolling gnocchi.

4. Cut dough into 8 equal parts, then use your hands to roll each part into a 14"-long roll. Cut rolls into ¾"-long pieces, forming plump pillow shapes. As you cut them, loosely scatter gnocchi (being careful not to let them touch one another) on a lightly floured, parchment-lined baking sheet.

5. Warm tomato sauce in a skillet over medium heat. Cook gnocchi in a large pot of gently simmering salted water over medium heat, stirring slowly with a wooden spoon to keep gnocchi from sticking together. When all gnocchi float to the surface, about 3 minutes, transfer with a slotted spoon into tomato sauce and gently toss together. Sprinkle with parmigiano-reggiano, if you like.

Italian Dumplings

G nocchi are dumplings—but while their eastern European cousins are usually made with white flour and water (and perhaps some kind of fat), Italy's gnocchi may be made with a number of different starches and assorted flavorings. Here are some of the most common varieties:

◆ **GNOCCHI DI PATATE:** By far the most popular gnocchi. There's some controversy over which varieties of potatoes are best for making gnocchi, but experts agree that they should be floury, not waxy.

◆ **GNOCCHI DI POLENTA:** From Tuscany, these cornmeal dumplings are generally made from leftover polenta, shaped into dumplings and tossed with meat or mushroom sauce.

◆ **GNOCS DI CACAO:** Savory rather than sweet, these are a tradition in Friuli, where they are served as a pasta course, not dessert. Friuli is also known for its gnocs di côce zale, or squash gnocchi (see page 114).

◆ **GNOCCHI DI PANE:** Developed to use up leftover bread, these dumplings resemble the knödel of Austria (known as canederli in Trentino-Alto Adige), usually served in broth—but are smaller and served instead in butter or tomato sauce.

◆ **GNOCCHI DI CASTAGNE:** These are made with chestnut flour—a traditional substitute for white flour in the poor mountain areas of Italy, where chestnuts have historically been an important food for the poor.

Naked Dinner

I n his *Classic Techniques of Italian Cooking* (Fireside, 1989), Giuliano Bugialli (above) proposes that ravioli nudi—a Florentine invention—are a survivor of earlier times. "Originally," writes Bugialli, himself a native of Florence, "ravioli were a lighter type of gnocchi or dumpling. The cookbooks of the fourteenth through the eighteenth centuries have many, many types of dumplings called ravioli." Today, ravioli nudi are rare at home tables in Florence and have all but disappeared from restaurant menus.

Ravioli Nudi

(Spinach and Ricotta Dumplings)

SERVES 4

R ESEMBLING loosely packed, rougher-textured spinach gnocchi, these dumplings—which originated in Florence, like so many spinach dishes—are called "naked" because they are in effect a ravioli filling without the cloak of dough.

2 large bunches spinach, trimmed
½ lb. ricotta, drained
Yolks of 4 extra-large eggs
1 ½ cups freshly grated parmigiano-reggiano
½ tsp. grated lemon zest
Cayenne
Freshly grated nutmeg
Salt and freshly ground black pepper
1 tbsp. flour
¼ cup butter, melted

1. Cook spinach in a large pot of boiling salted water over medium-high heat for 10 minutes, then drain in a colander and refresh under cold running water. Place spinach in a clean kitchen towel and squeeze until leaves are completely dry. (If there is moisture left in the spinach, ravioli will fall apart during cooking.) Finely chop spinach.

2. Combine ricotta, egg yolks, 1 cup of the parmigiano, and the lemon zest in a large mixing bowl. Stir in spinach and season to taste with cayenne, nutmeg, and salt and pepper. Add flour and stir just until combined.

3. Bring a large pot of salted water to a simmer over medium heat. Wet hands (mixture will be sticky) and shape 1 tbsp. of mixture into a 1" ball. Drop ball into simmering water and cook until it floats to the top. If ball holds its shape, continue rolling remaining mixture. If ball falls apart, add another 1–2 tsp. flour to mixture and test again. (Don't add more flour than absolutely necessary, or the ravioli will toughen.)

4. Cook ravioli in batches. As they float to the top, transfer to a serving dish and cover with aluminum foil to keep them warm. Drizzle ravioli with butter and top with remaining parmigiano. Serve immediately.

Gnocchetti ai Calamaretti

(Baby Gnocchi with Baby Squid)

SERVES 4

YOU PROBABLY won't find baby squid in the U.S., but this delicate signature dish from Alle Testiere (left) in Venice is worth making with regular squid, as small as possible.

FOR GNOCCHETTI:
2 medium russet potatoes (about 1½ lbs.)
1 tsp. salt
½ cup flour
2 egg yolks

FOR SAUCE:
¼ cup extra-virgin olive oil
2 cloves garlic, peeled and chopped
1 lb. baby calamari, cleaned (see sidebar, right), with bodies cut into ½" rings
3 pinches ground cinnamon
Salt and freshly ground black pepper
¼ cup dry white wine
½ cup chopped fresh Italian parsley leaves

1. For gnocchetti, put potatoes in a medium pot, cover with cold water, season with salt, and cook over medium-high heat until easily pierced with a knife, about 45 minutes. Drain in a colander. Peel potatoes while still hot, then press through a potato ricer into a mound on a lightly floured surface. Sprinkle with salt, then allow to cool enough to handle.

2. Make a well in center of potatoes and sprinkle in flour. Add egg yolks, then knead and fold mixture with heels of your hands, using a pastry scraper to remove dough sticking to floured surface, until mixture comes together to form a smooth dough, 1–2 minutes. Add 3–4 tbsp. flour if dough is sticky. Do not overwork dough, or gnocchi will be tough. Set dough aside, clean surface of any dough, then lightly flour. Wash, dry, and flour your hands before rolling gnocchi.

3. Cut dough into 8 equal parts, then use your hands to roll each part into a 14"-long roll. Cut rolls into ¾"-long pieces, forming plump pillow shapes. As you cut them, loosely scatter gnocchi (not touching one another) on a lightly floured, parchment-lined baking sheet.

4. For sauce, heat oil in a large skillet over medium-high heat. Sauté garlic until golden, about 1 minute. Add calamari and cinnamon and season with salt and pepper. Sauté until juices evaporate, about 3 minutes. Add wine and ¼ cup water and reduce for 2–3 minutes. Add half the parsley.

5. Cook gnocchi in a large pot of gently simmering salted water over medium heat, stirring slowly with a wooden spoon, to keep gnocchi from sticking together. When all gnocchi float to surface, about 3 minutes, transfer with a slotted spoon into skillet with calamari sauce. Add remaining parsley and gently toss together.

Cleaning Calamari

Most squid, or calamari, come already cleaned, whether fresh or frozen. If you're lucky enough to find fresh squid just out of the water, however, follow these easy instructions. Cut off tentacles just above the eyes. Squeeze the cut end of the tentacles to remove and discard beak. Set tentacles aside. Using the flat side of a chef's knife, scrape along the body from the tail to the opening. Push out and discard entrails, being careful not to break the flesh. The skin is edible, so it can be left on or scraped off. Reach into the body, remove transparent quill, and discard.

Egg Pasta Basics

The Simili sisters, Margherita and Valeria, have been making pasta since they were children. They learned by watching their mother in the big kitchen of their family home in Bologna, and pasta making now comes to them as naturally as breathing. For those of us who didn't grow up in an Italian kitchen, however, making pasta can seem formidable. Composed of only flour and eggs or water, pasta leaves nowhere to hide. It takes practice to get the feel of the various stages of the process—like the moment the dough comes together and is no longer sticky, and the moment it becomes smooth enough to feed through the rollers of a pasta machine. Valeria Simili showed us how to make spinach pasta (right) for lasagne verdi al forno (see page 126) and other pastas. To make a basic egg pasta to serve 4, use 1 cup unbleached all-purpose flour to 2 large eggs. Follow steps 2 through 4 at right, omitting the spinach.

Pasta Verde

(Spinach Pasta)

MAKES 4 6"x18" SHEETS

THESE THIRTEEN step-by-step photographs are probably as close as most of us will ever come to a pasta-from-scratch cooking class with the Bolognese-based Simili twins. To prepare basic egg pasta, without spinach, see sidebar (left).

2 bunches spinach, trimmed
1 ½ cups unbleached all-purpose flour
2 large eggs

1. Put ¼ cup of water into a large pot and bring to a boil over medium-high heat. Add spinach and cook until completely wilted (**A**), about 3 minutes. Drain in a colander and, when cool enough to handle, squeeze out water (**B**). Finely chop spinach, then grind into a purée with a mortar and pestle, and set aside.

2. Sift flour into a mound on a clean surface (**C**). Use your hand to make a well in the center (**D**) and add spinach (**E**). Break each egg separately onto a plate or bowl (**F**), then add to well. (This allows you to check for bad eggs and keeps any bits of shell out of the pasta.) Lightly beat eggs and spinach together with a fork (**G**), then gradually incorporate flour from the inside edge of the well into spinach mixture (**H**). When dough becomes too stiff to work with the fork, knead flour into spinach mixture with both hands (**I**) until dough is no longer sticky. Form dough into a ball (**J**) and cover with a damp kitchen towel. Clean your surface, then dust with more flour.

3. Unwrap dough and knead with the heel of your hand until dough is smooth, about 5 minutes. Flatten dough so it will fit through the rollers of a hand-cranked pasta machine. Set rollers of the pasta machine at the widest setting, then feed pasta through rollers 3 or 4 times, folding and turning pasta until it is smooth and the width of the machine. Cut dough into 4 pieces (**K**).

4. Begin rolling pasta through machine, decreasing the settings, one notch at a time (do not fold or turn pasta). Roll pasta through each setting until you reach the second from the finest notch (**L**). Cover pasta with a damp kitchen towel to keep from drying out until ready to cut pasta into the shape that you need (**M**).

Ragù alla Bolognese

(Bolognese Meat Sauce)

MAKES ABOUT 5 CUPS

HOW BETTER to learn the secrets of bolognese sauce, for lasagne verdi al forno (see page 126) and other uses, than from the Simili sisters in Bologna itself? Ragù turns out to be more than a simple meat sauce; it includes prosciutto, chopped chicken livers, and the mellowing surprise of milk.

¼ cup extra-virgin olive oil

1 small yellow onion, peeled and minced

1 rib celery, minced

½ medium carrot, peeled and minced

2–3 slices prosciutto di Parma (about 3 oz.), finely chopped

2 chicken livers (about 3 oz.), finely chopped

1½ lbs. ground chuck

Salt and freshly ground black pepper

½ cup dry white wine

1 cup milk, hot

1 cup brodo di carne (see page 76), or beef broth

1 28-oz. can puréed Italian plum tomatoes

1. Heat oil in a large, deep, heavy pot over medium-high heat. Add onions and sauté until soft and translucent but not browned, 4–5 minutes. Add celery and carrot and cook for 3 minutes more. Add prosciutto and chicken livers and cook, stirring with a wooden spoon, until meat is just cooked and still a little pink. Crumble ground chuck into pot and season to taste with salt and pepper. Break up chuck, stirring constantly with the wooden spoon, until meat is just cooked and still a little pink, about 5 minutes more. (To keep meat tender, do not fry or brown.)

2. Stir in wine and cook until it evaporates completely, about 3 minutes. Reduce heat to medium and add hot milk, stirring occasionally, until milk has evaporated. Heat broth and tomatoes together in a small saucepan over medium-high heat until hot, then add to meat mixture. Reduce heat to low and gently simmer for 2½ hours, stirring occasionally. Season to taste with salt and pepper.

Béchamel or Balsamella

Although widely recognized by its French name, béchamel, this sauce has been known in Italy as balsamella (or besciamella, or bechimella) for centuries. The sauce functions as a binding element in many pasta and vegetable dishes. It is also used as a topping in baked dishes—most notably lasagne and cannelloni—to prevent them from drying out. To make 2 cups of béchamel, melt 3 tbsp. butter in a heavy medium saucepan over medium-low heat. Add 4 tbsp. sifted flour and whisk for 1½ minutes (do not allow to brown). Gradually add 2 cups hot milk, whisking constantly. Season to taste with salt and pepper and stir constantly until sauce is as thick as heavy cream, about 15 minutes.

Lasagne Verdi al Forno

(Baked Spinach Lasagne)

SERVES 8-12

THIS PERFECT Bolognese lasagne is a far cry from the weepy steam-table casseroles that so often pass for lasagne in America. Valeria Simili (far right, bottom) taught us how to make this excellent version in Bologna itself.

2 tbsp. extra-virgin
   olive oil
Salt
1 recipe spinach pasta
   (see page 122)
1 recipe ragù alla
   bolognese (see page
   125), about 5 cups
1 cup freshly grated
   parmigiano-reggiano
1 recipe béchamel sauce
   (see sidebar, page
   125), about 2 cups

1. Preheat oven to 450°. Lightly oil a 9" x 12" baking pan and set aside. Cook pasta sheets in a large pot of salted boiling water over high heat 2 sheets at a time until they float to the surface, about 10 seconds. Carefully remove with a slotted spoon and plunge into a large bowl of salted ice water to stop further cooking. Remove from water when cool and dry between two clean kitchen towels.

2. Line the bottom of prepared baking pan with a layer of pasta, trimming sheets with a knife so that they fit in one even layer (patch if necessary). Spread evenly with 1 cup of ragù (**A**), then sprinkle lightly with parmigiano (**B**). Add another layer of pasta (**C**), evenly spread 1 cup of béchamel on pasta, then sprinkle lightly with parmigiano (**D**). Repeat layers (you will have 3 layers of ragù and 2 of béchamel), ending with ragù (**E**) and parmigiano. Reserve any extra bolognese sauce for another use.

3. Bake in top third of the oven for 10 minutes. Turn oven up to 500° and cook until lasagne is bubbling around the edges and browned on top, 5–7 minutes more . Do not overcook. Allow lasagne to rest for 8–10 minutes before serving (**F**).

The Layered Look

The best-known baked Italian pasta is undoubtedly lasagne, which is of course wide pasta sheets layered with various ingredients, then put in the oven. Believed to date back at least to Roman times (its name may or may not derive from the Latin *lasania*, meaning "cooking pot"), and possibly to ancient Greece, lasagne has been widely adopted around the Italian peninsula, each region putting its own spin on the dish. In Bologna, for instance, lasagne is typically made with spinach pasta and moistened with classic meat-based ragù alla bolognese; in Liguria, lasagne is made with pesto (sometimes the sheets are boiled and then tossed with pesto instead of being layered as in the Genoese dish mandilli de sæa al pesto; see page 89); Neapolitans layer the pasta sheets with tomato sauce and mozzarella; Calabrians prefer ricotta salata.

127

Ravioli di Zucca

(Pumpkin Ravioli)

SERVES 6

FRANCESCO ANTONUCCI, Veneto-born chef at Remi in Manhattan, gave us this recipe. Cheese pumpkins—not jack-o'-lanterns—are the best American pumpkins to use.

FOR FILLING:
1 2½-lb. cheese pumpkin,
  seeds removed, cut into
  chunks
2 egg yolks, lightly beaten
2 tbsp. extra-virgin
  olive oil
1 small yellow onion,
  peeled and finely
  chopped
1 tsp. red pepper flakes
6 amaretti (Italian
  almond cookies), crushed
  into crumbs
1 tsp. ground cinnamon
¼ cup freshly grated
  parmigiano-reggiano
2 tbsp. honey
1 cup dry white wine
1 tsp. salt

FOR SAUCE:
6 tbsp. butter
18 fresh sage leaves,
  chopped

1 recipe egg pasta (see
  page 122), cut
  into 12 large squares

1. For filling, preheat oven to 350°. Bake pumpkin chunks on a lightly oiled baking sheet until tender, 30–45 minutes. Remove from oven and set aside for about 10 minutes. When cool enough to handle, remove and discard skin. Transfer pumpkin pulp to a mixing bowl, mash with a fork, then beat in egg yolks and set aside.

2. Heat oil in a large pan over medium heat. Add onions and sauté until soft, about 10 minutes. Add red pepper flakes, amaretti, cinnamon, 2 tbsp. of the parmigiano, honey, wine, and salt and cook for 3–4 minutes. Mix in pumpkin, cook for 2 minutes more, then transfer to a food processor or blender and purée until smooth. Return pumpkin mixture to the same pan, cover, and keep warm over low heat.

3. For sauce, heat butter in a small skillet over medium heat. Add sage and cook until butter is golden brown, about 10 minutes. Remove from heat and set aside.

4. Bring a pot of salted water to a boil over high heat, then reduce to a simmer. Carefully slip pasta squares into pot and cook until they rise to the surface, about 2–3 minutes (fresh pasta cooks much faster than dried). Use a large skimmer to remove pasta from the water. Drain well, then lay 1 square on each of 6 plates, spoon pumpkin filling onto squares, flattening it down with the back of a spoon, and cover with remaining pasta squares. Drizzle sage butter over each square, sprinkle with remaining parmigiano, and garnish with additional fresh sage leaves, if you like.

Squashing Pumpkins

A las, most of us remain slaves to jack-o'-lantern pumpkins and plain old pumpkin pie," says writer and food historian William Woys Weaver, a self-proclaimed pumpkin lover. He also points out that "all pumpkins are squash. Americans have just fallen into the habit of calling the big orange ones pumpkins." The term derives from the Old English *pompion*, which in turn comes from the Latin *pepo* and the older Greek *pepon*—both words used by the ancients for golden, sun-ripened melons. All squash and most gourds, cucumbers, and melons belong in the extensive genus *Cucurbitaceae*. To the European eye of the 1500s, New World squashes apparently looked more like melons than like the gourds that had been known in the Old World since the Bronze Age.

Stuffed Pasta

Tortellini is but one variety of stuffed pasta in Italy. The most famous version, of course, is ravioli—which exists in many forms and which may or may not be a Genoese invention. Here are four of Italy's other favorite stuffed pastas, each defined by its characteristic shape and filling:

◆ **ANOLINI:** Traditionally prepared in Parma, this 16th-century, half-moon-shaped pasta is typically stuffed with prosciutto, mortadella, bread crumbs, and parmigiano-reggiano. While the classic way to serve anolini is in a rich beef broth, they may also be simply tossed with butter and grated parmigiano. (Don't confuse these with the ring-shaped stuffed pasta called agnolini, a specialty of Mantua.)

◆ **CAPPELLETTI** (little hats): This pasta from Emilia-Romagna resembles a three-cornered hat in shape. Cappelletti have two traditional stuffings, one based on meat and the other mostly cheese.

◆ **PANSOTTI** (pot-bellied ones): From Liguria comes this triangle-shaped pasta filled with fresh seasonal herbs and vegetables—especially borage and swiss chard—and usually served in a sauce based on crushed walnuts.

◆ **TORTELLI** (little cakes): Shaped like elongated ravioli. In Lombardy, the pasta is typically stuffed with yellow squash and served as a traditional Christmas dish.

Tortellini in Brodo

(Tortellini in Broth)

THE SIMILI sisters like to make their tortellini tiny and delicate, dabbing a fingertip of meat stuffing onto squares of homemade pasta, then folding them quickly and deftly.

FOR FILLING:
5 oz. pork loin or shoulder
3 oz. sliced prosciutto, roughly diced
4 oz. sliced mortadella, roughly diced
½ cup freshly grated parmigiano-reggiano
1 egg, lightly beaten
Freshly ground nutmeg

FOR TORTELLINI:
1 recipe egg pasta (see sidebar, page 122)
1 recipe brodo di carne (see page 76), or 3 quarts chicken stock

1. For filling, cook pork in a small nonstick skillet over medium heat until it is cooked through, about 8 minutes, then set aside to let cool. Coarsely chop cooled pork, then put pork, prosciutto, and mortadella into the bowl of a food processor fitted with a metal blade, and process until finely chopped but not a paste. Transfer to a mixing bowl, add parmigiano, egg, and nutmeg, and mix well.

2. For tortellini, working with one sheet of pasta at a time (keep the rest covered with a damp kitchen towel while you work to keep it from drying out), lay it on a lightly floured surface. Use a pasta/pastry-cutting wheel (**A**) or a sharp, thin-bladed knife to cut the pasta into 1½" squares, discarding any trimmings. Cover pasta with a kitchen towel to keep it from drying out.

3. To fill tortellini, pinch off about 1 tbsp. of the filling and roll into a thin "cigar" (**B**). Holding cigar in one hand, pinch off about ¼ tsp. and smear it onto each pasta square. Pile up the squares on a plate, occasionally dusting lightly with flour, so that they stay moist but don't stick together (**C**).

4. Fold one corner of each pasta square diagonally over the filling, leaving about ¼" of the bottom edge exposed, then lightly pinch to seal. Wrap the two loose corners, slightly overlapping, around the tip of your little finger and press them together to close the circle. Fold up opposite corner to form a miniature napkin–like fold (**D**). Repeat process with all pasta squares.

5. To cook tortellini, bring brodo to a boil in a large pot over high heat. Drop in all the tortellini at once. Stir gently with a wooden spoon and cook until all tortellini float to the surface, about 8 minutes. Adjust seasoning before serving.

A B
C D

Cannelloni

SERVES 4–6

WE DEVELOPED this elegant, slightly simplified variation on cannelloni Rossini (named for the famous Italian composer, also a noted gourmet) in the SAVEUR kitchen.

2 tbsp. extra-virgin
 olive oil
1 small yellow onion,
 peeled and minced
1 clove garlic, peeled and
 minced
1 chicken liver, chopped
6 oz. boneless, skinless
 chicken thigh, chopped
6 oz. ground veal
6 oz. ground pork
Salt and freshly ground
 black pepper
Pinch freshly ground
 nutmeg
1 recipe béchamel
 (see sidebar, page 125)
⅓ cup freshly grated
 parmigiano-reggiano
Salt
1 recipe egg pasta (see
 page 122), cut into 12
 4" x 5" sheets
4 cups tomato sauce
 (see page 90, steps 1
 and 2)
2 tbsp. butter

1. Heat oil in a medium skillet over medium heat. Add onions and garlic and cook, stirring often with a wooden spoon, until onions are soft, about 5 minutes. Add chicken livers and mash to a paste with the back of the spoon. Add chicken, veal, pork, and season to taste with salt and pepper. Cook, stirring often, until meat is cooked through, about 10 minutes. Transfer meat to a cutting board and chop until texture is very fine and meat begins to hold together. Transfer meat to a medium bowl, stir in nutmeg, and set aside.

2. Warm béchamel in a medium saucepan over medium-low heat. Stir in about ¼ cup of the parmigiano (reserving some to use as topping). Add ½ cup of the warmed sauce to the meat mixture and set remaining béchamel aside.

3. Preheat oven to 375°. Cook pasta several sheets at a time in a large pot of boiling salted water over high heat until tender, about 30 seconds. Dip cooked pasta briefly in a large bowl of cold water. Lay sheets out, not touching, on clean, damp kitchen towels and cover with another damp towel.

4. Working with one sheet of pasta at a time, spread 2–3 tbsp. meat filling along wide edge, then roll up, jelly-roll style. Repeat with remaining pasta and filling.

5. Spread a thin layer, about 1 cup, tomato sauce over bottom of a large baking dish. Lay cannelloni, seam side down, in a single layer on top of tomato sauce. Spread another thin layer of tomato sauce over cannelloni. Spoon remaining béchamel over tomato sauce, sprinkle with remaining parmigiano, and dot with butter. Bake until sauce is bubbling, 15–20 minutes, then brown under broiler for 3–4 minutes.

Wine from the Fog

In south-central Piedmont, in the Langhe hills around the fabled town of Alba—cannelloni country—a grape called nebbiolo (the name is thought to be derived from the word *nebbia*, or fog, a meteorological phenomenon that tends to cloak the region's vineyards around the time of the harvest every fall) yields two of Italy's greatest wines: barolo and barbaresco. Nebbiolo has been planted in this area since at least the 13th century, but most experts agree that it wasn't until the 1800s, when Piedmont was under the reign of the French-born House of Savoy, that local wines first achieved high quality. Barolo, traditionally a hard, tannic wine known more for its vinous character than for anything resembling fruit, used to be considered a more "serious" wine than barbaresco. That distinction is largely meaningless today, however, and like barolo, barbaresco can be a luscious, grapey wine of great complexity.

Sicilian Complexity

The Sicilian larder is stocked with vividly flavored raw materials—herbs and spices (including chiles and saffron), citrus fruits, preserved fish in several forms, cheeses both native and imported from elsewhere in Italy. Sicilian cooks—whether French-influenced monzùs working for noble families, like Papa Andrea, grandfather of actor and cookbook author Vincent Schiavelli (above), or simple homemakers putting the nightly meal on the table—like to use such ingredients to make complex, often subtle dishes that can make northern Italian fare seem downright simplistic. Consider not just constructions like the timbale at right but also Sicily's elaborate impanata, a pie filled with various combinations of pork products, vegetables, or, in one case, eel and broccoli; or such pastas as penne with kippered herring and bottarga (dried mullet or tuna roe), spaghetti with chile-spiced bottarga and anchovy pesto, or the famous bucatini con le sarde (see page 102); or the elaborate seafood couscous, or cuscusù, that is one of the most eloquent Moorish legacies to Sicilian cuisine; or the countless rolled meats, croquettes, and savory pies that turn up as main courses on the tables of Sicily. It's all a long way from red sauce.

Tumala d'Andrea
(Sicilian Rice and Pasta Timbale)

SERVES 6

PAPA ANDREA, Vincent Schiavelli's grandfather, created this lighter—and surprisingly easy—version of the traditional tumala, an ancient, many-layered casserole.

2 cups arborio or other
   risotto rice
Salt
3 eggs
2 ½ cups grated pecorino
   romano
½ lb. ziti or penne rigate
2 cups tomato sauce
   (see page 90, steps
   1 and 2), warm
½ cup fresh shelled or
   frozen peas
½ cup dried bread crumbs
Freshly ground black
   pepper

1. Cook rice in a large pot of boiling salted water until al dente, about 15 minutes. Drain, then transfer to a large bowl. Allow rice to cool completely, then stir in 2 of the eggs and 1 cup of the pecorino. Cover with a dish towel and set aside in refrigerator for at least 6 hours.

2. Preheat oven to 400°. Cook pasta in a large pot of boiling salted water over high heat until not quite tender, about 8 minutes. Drain, transfer to a large bowl, and toss with 1 cup sauce. (It is important that sauce be thick, or pasta mixture will be too watery and tumala will fall apart when unmolded.) Add peas and ½ cup pecorino, then mix gently with a wooden spoon and set aside to let cool.

3. To assemble the tumala, coat the inside of a well-oiled 2-quart 8" ovenproof bowl with bread crumbs. Moisten hands so that rice and pasta won't stick to them, then completely line bowl with rice, forming an even wall about ½" thick. Gently pack pasta into bowl, then top with remaining rice, pressing it firmly in place. Lightly beat remaining egg, then brush over top of tumala.

4. Bake until tumala is golden, about 1 hour. Allow to cool for 10 minutes, then loosen sides with a knife. Turn out onto a large platter. (If necessary, tap bottom of bowl to loosen.) Slice into wedges at the table and serve topped with additional sauce, grated pecorino, and pepper.

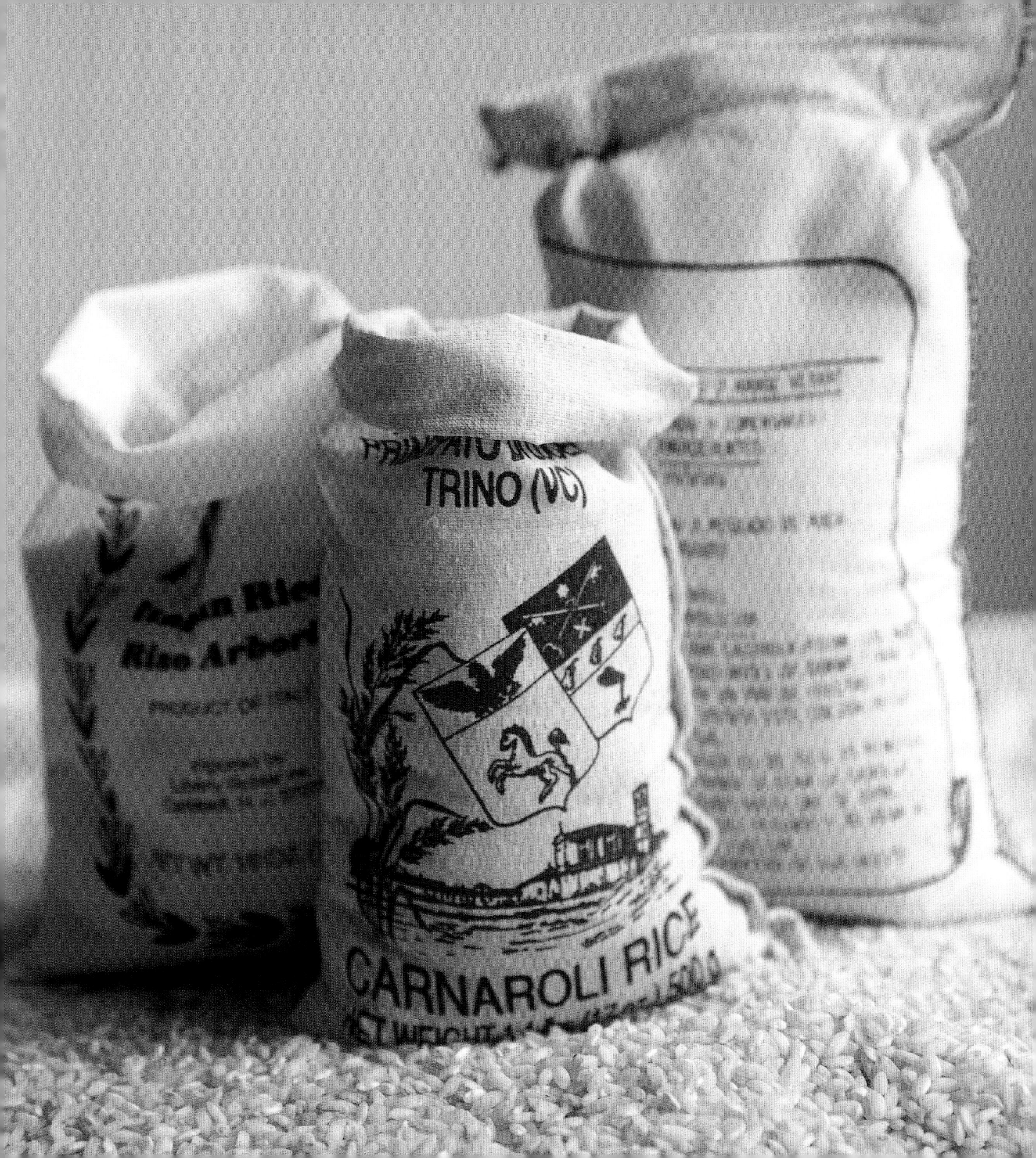
TRINO (VC)
CARNAROLI RICE

MARCELLA HAZAN ON
RISOTTO

RISOTTO HAS A REASON," says Marcella Hazan in that unmistakable voice, paved by a lifetime of Marlboros and of speaking her mind. Drawing us out of her tiny Venetian kitchen into a small study, Hazan (below right), not just a legendary cooking teacher and indispensable author but also a scientist with two advanced degrees, commands us to inspect three single grains of carnaroli rice: "Look carefully. Each grain has two starches: the translucent outside is amylopectin, the inside is amylose. They react differently to heat and moisture. The inside expands while the outside dissolves. That's why you must keep stirring risotto." ◆ "Carnaroli," she pronounces, "is the best rice for risotto. Look for the words *ai pestelli* on the package, which means it was hulled with a mechanical mortar and pestle, which leaves the rice covered with a powdery starch. You never wash the rice first because you need that starch to make it creamy. Carnaroli doesn't go from undercooked to overcooked in a second; it has more finesse than arborio, which caught on in America just be-

cause it was available." ◆ We watch as Hazan prepares risotto for us. "I never wait until the fat is hot," she says, adding vegetable oil, butter, and chopped onions all at once to a deep metal saucepan. "You can add broth—we don't have stock in Italy—water, anything," she continues. "It doesn't matter." (She often, in fact, uses bouillon cubes.) "What matters is that you do it right. That television chef, you know, he makes risotto in a frying pan!" She rolls her eyes mischievously. "You cannot make risotto in a frying pan. There's too much floor. It goes too fast. My students are always asking when to add liquid. When it's *dry*, I tell them. And no salt yet. I like salt, but the butter is salty. The broth is salty. Enough. And you cook it over *high* heat. The broth is always simmering." To the onions, she adds diced yellow peppers and blanched green beans. "When they're cooked they taste string beans," she says. "Before cooking they taste grass. In California they don't even cook their vegetables—they just show them the water." Then she sprinkles in the rice, and 15 minutes later the risotto is ready for us to sample.

Going with the Grain

The Italian short-grain rices vialone nano, carnaroli, and (most widely available of the three) arborio are all used for risotto in Italy. But they're also perfect for rice salads and other cold dishes. Unlike long-grain varieties, which tend to grow hard and chalky when cold, short-grain rices—with their high starch content—stay tender, chewy, and succulent, making them ideal for antipasti dishes like pomodori a riso (see page 27) and for even simpler preparations. "For these uses," explains SAVEUR executive editor Christopher Hirsheimer, "we don't portion out stock, risotto style. We simply cook the rice in a large pot of boiling salted water as if it were pasta, stirring often to prevent it from clumping. When it's tender, we drain it, then use it however we like. One of the easiest things of all to do with it is simply to dress it while it's still warm with fruity olive oil and lots of fresh herbs and season it to taste with salt and freshly ground black pepper." *Ottimo!*

Risotto coi Fagiolini Verdi e il Peperone Giallo

(Risotto with Green Beans and Yellow Bell Pepper)

SERVES 4–6

MARCELLA HAZAN prepared this risotto dish, which comes from her cookbook *Marcella Cucina* (HarperCollins, 1997), for us in her tiny, cannily designed kitchen atop a 16th-century house in the Cannaregio quarter of Venice.

½ lb. green beans, trimmed
Salt
1 beef bouillon cube
3 tbsp. butter
1 tbsp. vegetable oil
1 small yellow onion, peeled and finely chopped
1 yellow bell pepper, cored, seeded, and cut into ½" dice
1⅔ cups carnaroli or other risotto rice
⅔ cup freshly grated parmigiano-reggiano
Freshly ground black pepper

1. Blanch beans in a medium pot of boiling salted water for 2 minutes. Drain and cut into ½" lengths, then set aside.

2. Meanwhile, bring 6 cups of water to a boil in a medium pot over high heat. Reduce heat to low, add bouillon cube, and stir until dissolved. Keep broth warm over low heat.

3. Put 1½ tbsp. of the butter, the oil, and the onions into a medium heavy pot and cook over medium-high heat, stirring often, until onions are pale gold, about 7 minutes. Add peppers, increase heat to high, and cook for about 30 seconds, stirring constantly. Add reserved green beans and continue cooking, stirring often, for 3–4 minutes.

4. Add rice to the beans and peppers, stirring to coat with the oil and butter and to combine with vegetables. Add about ¾ cup of the simmering broth at a time, stirring the rice constantly; wait until almost all of the broth has been absorbed before adding more. Continue cooking and adding broth (you may have some broth left over) until rice is tender but firm to the bite, about 20 minutes.

5. Remove pot from heat and vigorously stir in remaining 1½ tbsp. butter and the parmigiano, then season liberally with salt and pepper. Transfer to a warm platter and serve immediately.

Risotto con Scampi e Radicchio

(Risotto with Scampi and Radicchio)

SERVES 4

IN AMERICA, *scampi* has come to mean a garlicky shrimp dish (see page 186). But scampi, featured in this risotto served at the Palazzo Brandolini in Venice, are actually salt-water lobsterette tails (*Nephrops norvegicus*)—also sold as Dublin Bay prawns. Fresh small shrimp may be substituted.

1 fish bouillon cube

3 tbsp. extra-virgin olive oil

1 small white onion, peeled and minced

2 cloves garlic, peeled and minced

1 ¼ lbs. small shrimp, peeled

1 ⅔ cups carnaroli or other risotto rice

1 cup tocai friulano or other dry Friuli white wine

1 medium radicchio di treviso, trimmed and chopped

1 tbsp. butter

¼ cup grated parmigiano-reggiano

Salt

1. Bring 5 cups water to a boil in a medium pot over high heat. Reduce heat to low, add bouillon cube, and stir until dissolved.

2. Heat oil in a medium heavy pot over medium-low heat. Add onions and garlic and cook, stirring often with a wooden spoon, until soft, about 10 minutes. Increase heat to medium-high, add shrimp, and cook for 1 minute.

3. Add rice, stir to coat well, then add wine and cook until alcohol evaporates, about 3 minutes. Add about ¾ cup of the simmering broth at a time, stirring the rice constantly; wait until almost all of the broth has been absorbed before adding more. Continue cooking and adding broth (you may have some broth left over) for about 20 minutes, then add radicchio. Continue cooking until rice is tender but firm, about 5 minutes more. Remove from heat, stir in butter and parmigiano, and season to taste with salt.

From the Terrace

Anyone who has been to Venice or has even seen it in the movies has probably fantasized about peeking inside—or peeking out of—one of the magnificent palaces that face the Grand Canal. We got the chance to do both not long ago when Brandino and Marie Brandolini—Count and Countess Brandolini, to be precise—invited us to lunch at their landmark 15th-century Palazzo Giustinian (left). Arriving there by water taxi, we entered through a cavernous ground-floor hallway and took an elevator upstairs. The Brandolinis welcomed us, first into their warmly furnished, quietly elegant living room, where the sunlight picked out masses of vivid orchids (grown by Brandino's father at Vistorta, the family wine estate in Friuli). Then we climbed a spiral staircase up to the terrace, where we nibbled cheese biscuits and sipped prosecco. Standing on top of this historic palace, we chattered about Venice and picked out familiar sights from an unfamiliar vantage point—the Campanile, the domes of the Basilica of San Marco, the sadly burnt-out shell of La Fenice, the opera house. Now, this was Venice in style.

Buying Truffles

White truffles are one of the most intensely aromatic—some people say stinky—foodstuffs known to humankind. They've been accused of smelling like everything from old gym socks to, well, sex—and their perfume is so pervasive that Italians forbid passengers to carry them on public transportation. That said, it is hardly surprising that the first rule for buying white truffles is: If it doesn't have a strong aroma, don't buy it. You should also look for truffles that are firm but not unyielding to the touch (they shouldn't feel spongy) and that are pale beige in color. Restaurateurs tend to prefer cosmetically perfect truffles, round and more or less smooth, but shape doesn't affect flavor. Avoid cracked, broken truffles, though, or any that are riddled with little holes. White truffles are now readily available in the U.S. in the late fall and early winter months, but they are inevitably very expensive. The good news is that a little truffle goes a long way.

Risotto di Funghi con Tartufi Bianchi

(Mushroom Risotto with White Truffles)

SERVES 4–6

IN LATE FALL and early winter—white truffle season—in Piedmont, restaurants on every level offer these precious, fragrant tubers "on the side", at a fixed price. For that amount, you may have a portion of truffle shaved directly onto your pasta or risotto or anything else. This risotto, incidentally, is very good even without the truffles.

½ oz. dried porcini
3 cups chicken stock
1–1 ½ tbsp. unsalted butter
2 large shallots, peeled and chopped
1 clove garlic, peeled and minced
2 fresh sage leaves, chopped
1 cup carnaroli or other risotto rice
½ cup chianti or other dry Italian red wine
½ lb. fresh wild mushrooms (e.g., chanterelles, morels, or porcini), cleaned and sliced
½ cup grated parmigiano-reggiano
Salt and freshly ground black pepper
1½–2 oz. fresh white truffles, or more

1. Soak dried porcini in 1 cup very hot water for 30 minutes. Remove porcini and reserve liquid. Rinse porcini thoroughly, drain well, chop coarsely, and set aside. Strain liquid through a fine sieve or coffee filter and set aside.

2. In a medium pot, bring stock to a boil over high heat, then reduce heat to low and keep stock warm over low heat.

3. Melt butter in a large saucepan over medium heat. Add shallots, garlic, and sage and cook, stirring occasionally, until shallots are translucent, 5–7 minutes. Add rice and cook, stirring constantly, until lightly toasted and coated with butter, about 5 minutes.

4. Add wine and cook until absorbed, stirring constantly, about 3 minutes. Stir in all the mushrooms, including reserved dried porcini, along with porcini liquid and ½ cup chicken stock. Maintaining a simmer, cook, stirring frequently, until liquid is almost absorbed, 3 to 5 minutes. Continue adding stock, about ¾ cup at a time, stirring frequently, until rice is tender but firm to the bite and mixture is creamy but not soupy, about 20 minutes.

5. Remove risotto from heat, stir in parmigiano, season to taste with salt and pepper, and serve immediately. Shave white truffles directly onto risotto at the table.

Milanese Gold

We've heard two stories as to why risotto alla milanese is colored and flavored with that ancient and expensive spice called saffron (zafferano in Italian). Both have to do with the decoration of Il Duomo, the beautiful cathedral in Milan's center. One story has it that mosaic artists in the late 14th century, using gold leaf profligately in their work on the edifice, liked to lord it over other craftsmen by crumbling the precious metal into their rice. The use of saffron, it is said, was a slightly more affordable echo of this practice. A more elaborate and specific story says that an apprentice to the 16th-century Flemish painter Valerio da Perfundavalle, who was restoring the Duomo's stained-glass windows and had a habit of enriching his yellows with saffron, was given the nickname Zafferano—and that when this lad got married, his friends stirred saffron into the risotto as a prank. The amazing thing about such tales is that they never seem to admit the possibility that perhaps an early Milanese cook with a wealthy patron and a healthy imagination simply figured out that saffron added wonderful flavor and aroma to the dish.

Risotto alla Milanese
(Milanese-Style Risotto)

SERVES 6

IN THE CANVAS-tented courtyard of Don Lisander in Milan, owners Luigi Lucchini and Luigi Toffalori serve this impeccable risotto with osso buco (see page 224).

6 cups brodo di carne (see page 76) or beef stock
3 pinches saffron
3 tbsp. butter
1 tbsp. extra-virgin olive oil
1 small yellow onion, peeled and finely chopped
1 cup carnaroli or other risotto rice
1 tbsp. dry white wine
½ cup freshly grated parmigiano-reggiano
Salt

1. Bring 5 cups of the stock to a boil in a medium pot over high heat. Reduce heat to low and keep stock warm. Meanwhile, warm the remaining 1 cup of stock in a small pot over medium heat and crumble in saffron. Reduce heat to low and keep stock warm. Put 1 tbsp. of the butter, the oil, and onions into a medium heavy pot and cook over medium-high heat, stirring often, until onions are pale gold, about 7 minutes.

2. Add rice to pot, stirring to coat with oil and butter. Add wine and cook for 1 minute. Add 1 cup of the simmering stock at a time, stirring the rice constantly; wait until almost all of the stock has been absorbed before adding more. When larger pot of stock is about halfway empty, add saffron-infused stock and continue cooking and stirring. When it has been absorbed, continue adding plain stock (you may have some left over) until rice is tender but firm to the bite, about 20 minutes.

3. Remove pot from heat and vigorously stir in remaining 2 tbsp. butter and parmigiano, then season to taste with salt.

From the Lagoon

The lagoon surrounding Venice is a remarkable ecosystem, self-sustaining, self-renewing, teeming with fish and shellfish—and also yielding, from the little farm plots and gardens on some of its smaller, lesser-known islands, a wealth of flavorful produce. "The best things you can eat in Venice," Arrigo Cipriani of the city's famed Harry's Bar once told us, "come from the lagoon—not just the seafood but the vegetables. Because of the slightly salty ground, things grown on the islands have a special character." Sailing around the most celebrated of the garden islands, Sant'Erasmo, northeast of Venice itself, we saw almost no buildings—just low stone walls inset here and there with drainage channels, and behind them low vineyards and rows and rows of spiky artichoke plants. We could almost taste the salt air and smell the growing vegetables.

Risi e Bisi
(Rice and Peas)

SERVES 4

A STAPLE of Venetian cooking, this quasi-risotto appears in the city every spring, often made with the superlative peas grown on Sant'Erasmo, an island in the lagoon famous for its market gardens. This recipe comes from Mara Martin (left) at Da Fiore, one of our favorite restaurants in Venice.

2 lbs. fresh peas in pods
Salt
4 tbsp. butter
2 oz. pancetta, diced
1 small yellow onion, peeled and minced
2 tbsp. extra-virgin olive oil
1⅓ cups carnaroli or other risotto rice
Freshly ground black pepper
½ bunch Italian parsley leaves, minced
½ cup freshly grated parmigiano-reggiano

1. Shell peas, reserving pods. Place pods in a medium pot with 8 cups lightly salted water. Bring to a boil over high heat, reduce to medium-low, and simmer for 1 hour. Strain broth into a medium pot, pressing on pods. Discard pods. Keep broth warm over low heat.

2. Melt 2 tbsp. of the butter in a large, heavy pot over medium heat. Add pancetta and onions and cook, stirring with a wooden spoon, until onions are golden, about 10 minutes. Add peas and ½ cup warm broth. Cover and cook until peas are tender, 5–10 minutes.

3. Increase heat to high, uncover, and cook off any remaining liquid. Add oil. When oil is hot, add rice and stir to coat well. Add about ¾ cup warm broth and cook, stirring constantly, until most of the broth has been absorbed. Add about ¾ cup more broth. Continue cooking, stirring and adding broth as needed, until rice is tender but firm to the bite, about 20 minutes. Remove from heat and season to taste with salt and pepper. Stir in 1 more cup broth, remaining 2 tbsp. butter, parsley, and ¼ cup parmigiano (risi e bisi should be slightly soupier than ordinary risotto). Cover and allow to rest for a few minutes. Serve with additional parmigiano.

LIDIA BASTIANICH ON
POLENTA

POLENTA IS A FOOD that hugs you and comforts you and earns you praise at the table," writes Lidia Bastianich, the New York–based restaurateur and TV personality (see page 161), in her cookbook *Lidia's Italian Table* (William Morrow, 1998). In person, Bastianich (below right) happily expands on polenta's appeal. "I love the texture. We Italians are very tactile when it comes to food—the phrase 'al dente' doesn't come out of the blue sky, you know—and I especially like coarsely ground yellow polenta. It rakes my mouth somehow, cleans it, and then I'm ready for another mouthful of sausage or cheese or whatever." Widely eaten in Bastianich's native Istria (now in Croatia, but long part of Italy), polenta has been a basic foodstuff in the region since the late 17th century and has precedents in the grain porridges of the Romans. ◆ Polenta is a simple dish—just cornmeal and water, simmered into a soft mass. Traditionally, the simmering was done in a heavy brass or iron pot to prevent the meal from scorching. Bastianich remembers her grandmother making polenta in such a cauldron, hung on two thick chains over a hearth fire. "With a long wooden spatula," she tells us, "Grandma would mix the perking polenta—it looked like bubbles of exploding lava in the mouth of a volcano. When the polenta was poured out of the cauldron, a thin layer always remained attached to the sides. With the heat of the cauldron, it would dry and turn into a kind of corn chip. We children would wait for Grandma to pour out the polenta, then peel it away. Our fingertips would occasionally pay a price, but it was well worth it." We watch Bastianich pour out her polenta as her grandmother used to do, onto a round board, where it sits, stiffening, for a few moments. Then she slices the craggy yellow mound with a string suspended between tiny handles, gently passing it beneath the polenta and then lifting up and pulling through (facing page). The warm, dense slices make a good bed for meat ragù, but they may also be grilled, baked, pan-fried, even steamed. Spooned soft from the pot and topped with sugar and milk, polenta makes a fine breakfast, too. "For me," Bastianich says, "polenta fits every meal."

Grits all'Italiano

Cornmeal mush is popular in several corners of the world, including the American South, where it is known as grits; Romania, where it goes by the name mamaliga; and, of course, northern Italy—where, as polenta, it is the basic starch for Friuli, the Veneto, and some neighboring precincts. The Friulians have historically consumed so much of it, in fact, that they are sometimes called *polentoni*—big polenta eaters. Polenta tends to intimidate cooks who haven't grown up making it, but it is really quite easy to master—and worth the trouble. Polenta comes in yellow and white versions and in coarse and fine grinds. The yellow has an intense corn flavor, while the white—which Venetians prefer—is more delicate. And instant polenta? "A perversion!" exclaims Cesare Benelli of Al Covo in Venice. "It's cooked and dehydrated—like powdered mashed potatoes!" On the other hand, you don't necessarily need to use expensive Italian cornmeal when polenta is called for. When Veneto-born American-radicchio grower Lucio Gomiero and his wife made us a variation on ribollita—thickened with polenta instead of dried bread—at their home in California, they blithely poured in Albers yellow cornmeal, and the results tasted very good indeed.

Polenta

SERVES 6

TRADITIONALISTS, among them Istrian-born Lidia Bastianich, recommend sifting polenta through your fingers into boiling, salted water, whisking all the while—but, frankly, we've had better luck adding it all at once to cold water while vigorously whisking. Stirring the polenta constantly as it cooks becomes more difficult as it thickens—but it is important to prevent a crust from forming.

1 tbsp. coarse salt
2 bay leaves
1 ⅔ cups coarse polenta (yellow or white cornmeal)
1 tbsp. extra-virgin olive oil
Salt and freshly ground black pepper

1. Add salt and bay leaves to 7 cups of cold water in a medium pot, then stir in polenta.

2. Bring to a boil over high heat and add olive oil. Reduce heat to medium-low and continue cooking, stirring constantly with a wooden spoon, until polenta thickens and pulls away from the bottom and sides of the pot, 30–40 minutes. Season to taste with salt and pepper. Remove and discard bay leaves before serving

VARIATION—To grill or fry polenta, follow steps 1 and 2. Rinse a medium ceramic or glass baking dish with water, pour hot polenta into wet dish, and set aside to let cool. Place a large plate on top of baking dish and invert polenta onto plate. Cut into pieces with a wet knife. Grill on a very hot, dry grill or sear in a nonstick skillet until golden brown.

Polenta al Sugo

(Polenta with Meat Sauce)

SERVES 6

ALTHOUGH polenta is more common in northeastern Italy, it is also appreciated in Tuscany. We encountered this simple but slightly upscale presentation, with a sauce based on ground veal, at I Ricchi in Cercina, near Florence.

⅓ cup extra-virgin olive oil

1 medium yellow onion, peeled and finely diced

2 ribs celery, finely diced

2 small carrots, peeled and finely diced

2 lbs. ground veal

Salt and freshly ground black pepper

1 cup chianti or other dry Italian red wine

4 tbsp. tomato paste

1 recipe polenta (see page 150)

1. Heat oil in a medium heavy-bottomed pot over medium-high heat. Add onion and sauté, stirring with a wooden spoon, until soft and translucent, 4–5 minutes. Add celery and carrots and continue stirring until soft, about 3 minutes more.

2. Crumble ground veal into pot and season to taste with salt and pepper. Stir constantly, breaking up meat with the wooden spoon, until veal is just cooked and a little pink, about 5 minutes more (to keep meat tender, do not fry or brown).

3. Add wine and cook, stirring occasionally, until it has evaporated, 5–6 minutes. Add tomato paste and 4 cups of water and bring to a boil. Reduce heat to low and gently simmer until meat is tender and sauce has thickened, about 3 hours. Adjust seasoning and serve sauce spooned on top of polenta.

I Ricchi

When summer arrives in Tuscany, fashionable Florentines abandon the city heat for nearby shady hill towns—like Cercina, just north of Florence. In 1929, Umberto Consigli built a home in the village (above) for his family and opened a *bottega d'alimentari*, a neighborhood food shop, in one portion of the building. Out of their big kitchen, Consigli's wife, Cesarina, and her mother, Nonna Maria, would cook traditional Tuscan fare, like bistecca alla Fiorentina and fried sweetbreads, often inviting visitors to stay. After the Consiglis' daughter Irma married Biagio Ricchi, she took over the kitchen. "When Irma started cooking, people started dropping by deliberately around lunchtime, and soon the Ricchis decided to open a restaurant there," according to Chris Ricchi—who ran the establishment that became known as I Ricchi for 17 years along with her then husband Francesco (one of Biagio's and Irma's sons) and now owns an offshoot in Washington, D.C. The food remains simple; one specialty is a fritto misto which includes fried rabbit and squash blossoms (see page 207).

Something Wild

Italians are arguably Europe's greatest mushroom lovers, and they demonstrate their passion enthusiastically, especially in the north, each fall. The most popular of all wild mushrooms in Italy are the earthy funghi porcini (*Boletus edulis*; cèpes in French; below), literally "piglet mushrooms"—perhaps for their meaty flesh—which are eaten fresh in season (even sometimes raw and thinly sliced in salad form) and dried the rest of the year (a mere ounce or two of reconstituted porcini secchi can add deep flavor to sauces and stews). Also prized, but much rarer in Italy, are morels, chanterelles, and—rarest of all—the delicately flavored ovuli (*Amanita caesarea*). The all-purpose way of cooking any mushroom, wild or cultivated, is as funghi trifolati (see page 254).

Polenta con Funghi
(*Polenta with Mushrooms*)

SERVES 4

P O R C I N I are essential for this dish, which we tasted at Don Lisander in Milan. The restaurant also uses chiodini (*Armillariella mellea*) and galletti or finferli (*Cantharellus cibarius*; chanterelles), but any wild mushrooms—and even cultivated varieties (like shiitakes) may be substituted.

FOR PORCINI:
8 small–medium fresh porcini, cleaned with a damp paper towel, tough stem ends trimmed
4 tbsp. extra-virgin olive oil
Salt and freshly ground black pepper
¼ cup. thinly sliced pieces parmigiano-reggiano
1 clove garlic, peeled and minced

FOR OTHER MUSHROOMS:
½ lb. fresh wild mushrooms, cleaned with a damp paper towel, tough stem ends trimmed
2 tbsp. extra-virgin olive oil
2 shallots, peeled and minced
1 sprig fresh Italian parsley, minced
¼ cup dry white wine
Salt and freshly ground black pepper

Half recipe polenta, sliced and fried (see variation, page 150)
Leaves from 1 small sprig fresh mint, minced

1. For porcini, preheat oven to lowest setting. Warm 2 tbsp. of the oil in a large non-stick skillet over medium-high heat. Thinly slice 4 of the porcini lengthwise (don't worry if pieces crack or crumble) and sauté until soft and golden, about 2 minutes. Season with salt and pepper, transfer to a warm platter, and sprinkle with cheese. Keep warm in the oven. Slice remaining 4 porcini in half. Heat remaining 2 tbsp. of the oil in the same skillet over medium-high heat, add garlic and porcini, and sauté until porcini are evenly caramelized around edges, turning often, about 5 minutes. Season with salt and pepper. Transfer to platter.

2. For other mushrooms, slice mushrooms, depending on their size, into even-sized pieces. Warm oil in the same skillet over medium-high heat. Add shallots and cook until soft, about 2 minutes. Add mushrooms and cook until golden, about 5 minutes. Add parsley and wine and cook until wine evaporates, about 3 minutes, then season to taste with salt and pepper. Remove and discard bay leaf, then transfer mushrooms to platter with porcini.

3. Divide fried polenta between 4 warm plates, then divide mushrooms evenly between the 4. Sprinkle mint over mushrooms and polenta. Lightly drizzle polenta with additional extra-virgin olive oil, if you like.

CHEESE AND EGGS

"TRUE mozzarella di bufala, made from

the milk of water buffalo, is succulent, soft,

and lightly briny—a delicacy. The version

made in Fondi, near Naples, by Giovanni Buonanno (near right) may be the best in Italy. 'But,' Buonanno warns, 'it's not something to eat after three or four days. Come to Fondi and eat it fresh.'" —WILLIAM MURRAY

Frico

(Friulian Cheese Crisps)

TRADITIONAL lunchtime fare for vineyard workers in Friuli, in northeastern Italy, frico is best made with the sweet Friulian cow's-milk cheese called montasio, sometimes available in America, but asiago makes a good substitute.

¼ lb. montasio or asiago, cut into rough pieces
¼ lb. parmigiano-reggiano, cut into rough pieces

1. Put montasio or asiago pieces into the bowl of a food processor fitted with a metal blade and process until finely ground, then transfer cheese to a medium bowl and set aside. Put parmigiano into the same bowl of the food processor, and process until finely ground. Combine parmigiano with other cheeses and stir to mix well.

2. Heat a large, nonstick skillet over medium-high heat. Sprinkle about ¼ cup cheese over bottom of pan. Cheese will begin to melt, then bubble and brown on edges. Use a fork to lift edges and loosen frico from the pan. When the surface has dried out slightly, use fork to help flip cheese onto an overturned drinking glass to let cool in a rough concave shape. Frico may be prepared several hours before serving.

Istrian Roots

New York–based restaurateur, cookbook author, and TV personality Lidia Bastianich—proprietor of Felidia and Becco in Manhattan (and Lidia's in Kansas City)—was born on the Istrian Peninsula, a triangle of land extending down into the Adriatic just east of Venice. At the time of her birth, Istria was Italian territory; after World War II, it became part of Yugoslavia; today, it is Croatia. As far back as Bastianich (above, with her granddaughter Olivia) can remember, she helped in the kitchen, especially at her grandparents' houses in the town of Busoler. She remembers shaping gnocchi and drying herbs with her great-aunt Santola Maria; picking sea urchins, periwinkles, and mussels off the rocks with her brother, Franco; and eating Sunday lunch—fresh pasta, roasted meats, vegetables from the garden—under a fig tree in the family courtyard. "Those flavors, those aromas, are my reference points," she told SAVEUR deputy editor Margo True when True accompanied her on a pilgrimage back to Busoler in the late 1990s. "Some people are ashamed of their roots, but not me. This is my richness."

The Great Buffalo

L ittle is known about the origins of the water buffalo in Italy, except that it came somehow from India more than a millennium ago. Some say it was introduced here by the barbarian leader Agilulph in 596. Others claim that the Arabs transported buffalos to Sicily in the eighth or ninth century and that the Normans brought them up into the rest of Italy around the year 1000. What is certain is that by the 12th century, the beasts were being used as draft animals in various corners of the peninsula and that they were particularly useful for plowing marshy terrain, both because of their strength and because their huge hooves didn't sink easily into damp soil. It is not known who discovered that the animal's milk was especially sweet and well suited to cheese making, but the first mention of mozzarella di bufala dates from the 1400s. Incidentally, nobody uses mozzarella di bufala on pizza (or in mozzarella in carozza) in Naples; it's considered far too delicate—and expensive. Plain cow's-milk mozzarella does just fine.

Mozzarella in Carrozza
(Fried Mozzarella Sandwiches)

SERVES 6

UNLIKE THE clichéd mozzarella sticks found in American diners, this Italian original—literally, "mozzarella in a carriage" (i.e., the bread)—is *not* served with marinara sauce. Although traditionally only mozzarella is used as filling, this recipe from Casale in Rome adds prosciutto and anchovies, giving the dish a balance between salty and sweet.

12 very thin slices
   white bread
¼–½ lb. fresh
   mozzarella, sliced ¼"
   thick
3 thin slices prosciutto
3 anchovy filets
1 cup flour
2 eggs, beaten
1 cup dried bread crumbs
Extra-virgin olive oil

1. Lay out 6 slices of bread on a cutting board. Cut six 2" rounds out of mozzarella and place 1 round in the middle of each slice of bread. Tear prosciutto into 6 pieces approximately 2" square and lay one on top of each piece of cheese. Put half an anchovy filet on top of each piece of prosciutto and top with the remaining slices of bread. Press down on each sandwich with your palm and, using a 3" round cookie cutter, cut sandwiches into circles, discarding the scraps. The mozzarella and prosciutto should be pocketed within the bread.

2. Put the flour, eggs, and bread crumbs into separate small bowls. Carefully dip one sandwich at a time into first flour, then eggs, and finally bread crumbs, pinching the edges together. Roll edges of sandwiches through eggs and bread crumbs again if they do not appear to seal.

3. Pour oil into a large sauté pan to a depth of ½" and heat over medium-high heat until hot but not smoking, about 375° on a candy thermometer. Fry sandwiches until golden brown, carefully turning them over once, about 1 minute each side. Remove from oil, drain on paper towels, then transfer to a serving platter.

Frittate di Carciofi e Cipolle

(*Artichoke and Onion Omelettes*)

SERVES 6

UNLIKE French omelettes, frittate are fried on both sides. This basic recipe can be adapted to virtually any cooked vegetable—and frittate may also be filled with cooked pasta.

6 *tbsp. extra-virgin olive oil*
2 *medium yellow onions, peeled, halved, and sliced about ⅛" thick*
Salt and freshly ground black pepper
4 *large globe artichokes*
Juice of half a lemon
8 *eggs*

1. Heat 3 tbsp. of the olive oil in a 12" nonstick pan over medium heat. Add onions and fry until soft and translucent, about 10 minutes. Season with salt and pepper. Increase heat to medium-high and continue to cook until onions begin to caramelize, about 5 minutes more.

2. Meanwhile, bend back short lower leaves of artichokes until they snap, leaving the meaty bottom parts of the leaves. Cut off stems and slice off remaining cones of leaves, right above the hearts. Scrape out and discard the hairy chokes with a sharp spoon or melon baller. Cut artichokes into thick slices, transfer to a bowl, and squeeze lemon juice over them to prevent discoloration.

3. Use a slotted spoon to transfer cooked onions to a bowl, and set aside. In the same pan, heat another 2 tbsp. of the oil over medium-high heat, add artichokes, and sauté until soft and caramelized around the edges, about 15 minutes. Add onions to artichokes and toss together over the heat.

4. Beat eggs in a bowl with a fork until fluffy, season to taste with salt and pepper, then pour into pan over vegetables. Using a rubber spatula, stir quickly for a few seconds to mix eggs throughout, shake the pan, then let it settle to set and lightly brown the bottom. Run spatula around edge of pan and under edge of the frittata. Shake pan to loosen the frittata. Cook over medium-high heat for 2–3 minutes.

5. Remove pan from heat and cover with a plate larger than the pan. Using a kitchen towel, hold plate down tightly onto the pan and flip frittata over onto the plate. In the same pan, heat remaining 1 tbsp. of oil over medium heat. Slide frittata back into pan, uncooked side down, and cook until bottom has browned, 2–3 minutes. Serve warm.

Frittata Talk

I t is an indication of how ubiquitous the simple frittata is on the Italian table that the term itself has a vigorous folk life, in descriptive phrases and proverbs alike. Here are a few of them:

◆ FRITTATA By itself, the word is sometimes used to describe a multiple-car accident.

◆ FARE UNA FRITTATA To make a frittata—in other words, to make a mess of something or do something disastrous.

◆ RIGIRARE LA FRITTATA To flip a frittata over—that is, to turn around an argument.

◆ ORMAI LA FRITTATA È FATTA The frittata is already made; i.e., the situation is irreversible.

◆ NON SI PUÒ FAR LA FRITTATA SENZA ROMPERE LE UOVA You can't make an omelette without breaking the eggs—a proverb also known in English, meaning simply that to get the best results you have to pay a price.

Meltingly Good

The Piedmontese dialect word *fonduta*, like the French word *fondue*, simply means "melted"—although both refer specifically, in a culinary sense, to melted cheese. Fonduta and fondue aren't quite the same thing, however. Consider these significant differences between the two:

◆ FONDUTA is traditionally made with sweetish fontina cheese, not pungent, nutty gruyère, the typical basis of fondue.

◆ FONDUE is liquefied with white wine and a bit of kirsch; fonduta contains no alcohol and is diluted with milk in which the cheese has first been soaked.

◆ FONDUTA is made with eggs as well as cheese; although some French fondue recipes include eggs, too, the classic Swiss version does not.

◆ FONDUE is kept warm in a pot over a small flame and eaten on cubes of bread dipped into the molten cheese; fonduta is eaten straight from individual serving dishes, with a fork or spoon—sometimes with white truffles shaved over the top.

Fonduta

(Piedmontese Fondue)

SERVES 4–6

FONTINA from the alpine reaches of the Valle d'Aosta, Italy's smallest region, is traditional for this dish, but fontal—in effect, non-appellation fontina—may be substituted.

10 oz. fontina or fontal,
 rind trimmed, cut into
 small dice
1 cup milk
4 tbsp. butter
4 large egg yolks

1. Put cheese and milk into a small bowl (add more milk if necessary to just cover cheese), cover, and set aside overnight.

2. Bring water in the bottom half of a double boiler to a simmer over medium heat. Put butter into top half of double boiler. When it has melted, stir in cheese and milk until cheese has melted.

3. Add egg yolks to cheese mixture one at a time, whisking constantly with a small whisk, until sauce is smooth, thick, and glossy, about 10 minutes. Pour the fonduta into a warmed serving dish and serve immediately.

SEAFOOD

"THE VENETIAN table is laden with fish

and shellfish, much of it caught in the

surrounding waters and sold at the city's

extraordinary fish market, La Pescaria—

three kinds of clams; more than a dozen

sizes and shapes of squid and its relations; sweet gray shrimp and true scampi; two kinds each of mullet and turbot; eels and spider crabs and dogfish.... Truly local seafood is labeled *nostrani*, 'ours', a term that seems to define the whole cuisine." —COLMAN ANDREWS

RECIPES

CALAMARI ALLA PIASTRA *(Squid on the Griddle)*, page 173; GRANCEOLA CON ZUCCHINE E CARCIOFI *(Spider Crab with Zucchini and Artichokes)*, page 174; GAMBERONI GRIGI AL GRATIN *(Gratinéed Large Gray Shrimp)*, page 177; SEPPIE IN UMIDO COL NERO DI SEPPIA *(Cuttlefish Stewed in Its Ink)*, page 178; BACCALÀ MANTECATO *(Creamed Stockfish)*, page 181; SARDE IN SAOR *(Marinated Sardines)*, page 182; FRITTO MISTO *(Mixed Fried Seafood and Vegetables)*, page 185; SHRIMP SCAMPI *(Scampi-Style Shrimp)*, page 186; CACCIUCCO *(Livorno-Style Fish Stew)*, page 189.

Calamari alla Piastra

(Squid on the Griddle)

SERVES 4

ISTRIAN-BORN, New York–based chef and restaurateur Lidia Bastianich, who gave us this recipe, remembers catching squid with her uncle as a girl, attracting them with a light and strips of white cloth. In her *Lidia's Italian Table* (William Morrow and Company, 1998), she writes: "Soon the first calamari appeared, waving their tentacles and looking like puffs of pink smoke floating in the water. My uncle quickly threw the snag in like a lasso, and then with a splash, the calamari were landed in the boat."

2 lbs. fresh squid, cleaned (see sidebar, page 121), with skin and tentacles left on
½ cup extra-virgin olive oil
8 cloves garlic, peeled and sliced
Leaves from 1 branch fresh thyme
1 tsp. red pepper flakes
1 tsp. fine sea salt

1. Combine squid, oil, garlic, thyme, red pepper flakes, and salt in a medium bowl and marinate for 30 minutes.

2. Heat a large cast-iron griddle or skillet over medium-high heat. Transfer squid and marinade to hot griddle and immediately place the clean bottom of a medium cast-iron skillet directly on top of squid to flatten it as it cooks. Be sure skillet does not trap steam, or squid won't be crisp. Cook, turning squid once, until browned and crispy and juices have caramelized, about 8 minutes per side.

3. Transfer squid and juices to a large platter and serve garnished with parsley sprigs and wedges of lemon, if you like.

Squid School

There's more than one cephalopod in the sea. Here are the five most commonly used in Italy:

- ◆ **CALAMARI** (*Loligo vulgaris*). Your basic squid, about 4 to 6 inches long, but sometimes considerably larger or smaller (in general, the smaller ones are tastier).
- ◆ **CALAMARETTI.** Baby squid, generally around an inch and a half in length.
- ◆ **SEPPIE** (*Sepia officinalis*). Cuttlefish or inkfish, rounder than squid, with thicker flesh, more ink, and more flavor, too.
- ◆ **SEPPIETTE OR SEPPIOLINE** (*Sepiola rondeleti*). No more than about 2 inches long, this "baby cuttlefish" looks and tastes like the big one but is of a whole different species.
- ◆ **TOTANI** (*Todarodes sagitatus*). Flying squid, twice as big as a standard calamaro, with a tougher texture and larger tentacles. Usually stuffed.

Venetian Lifeblood

Everybody who comes to Venice," says Mauro Stoppa, "knows the canals. But they almost never notice the lagoon." To try to remedy that situation, he sails—and cooks—on the waters that flow through and around Venice aboard his boat, the *Eolo*. An agronomist by training, Stoppa was born south of the city, near Chioggia—the area's main fishing town—and has sailed, fished, and hunted on the lagoon all his life. In hopes of fostering greater respect for these waters, which are the lifeblood of Venice, Stoppa bought a 53-year-old, 52½-foot *bragasso*, a traditional-style fishing boat whose design dates back to the days of the doges. He restored and upgraded the craft, named it for the Greek god of wind, and started taking people—both locals and tourists—out on food-and-lore cruises. Stoppa's sisters Lucia and Julia (facing page, from left) help him prepare his lagoon-based meals.

Granceola con Zucchine e Carciofi

(Spider Crab with Zucchini and Artichokes)

SERVES 4

SPIDER CRAB (*Maja squinado*) is highly regarded in and around Venice. It is often served simply dressed with olive oil, but Mauro Stoppa—the captain and galley master of the *Eolo*, which plies the Venetian lagoon—remembers this preparation his mother used to serve when he was growing up.

6 small artichokes
7 tbsp. extra-virgin
   olive oil
2 medium zucchini,
   trimmed and sliced
   into thin rounds
1 scallion, trimmed and
   minced
2 cups fresh bread crumbs
2 sprigs fresh thyme, leaves
   minced
¼ bunch Italian parsley,
   trimmed and chopped
Salt and freshly ground
   black pepper
1 lb. jumbo lump crabmeat
Juice of 1 lemon

1. Pull off the tough green outer leaves of the artichokes until you reach the tender, mostly yellow leaves. Trim stems and slice about 1" off top of artichokes and use scissors to snip off the thorny tips of the leaves. Spread open leaves and scoop out fibrous white chokes with a spoon. Slice artichokes lengthwise into thin wedges.

2. Heat 4 tbsp. of the oil in a large skillet over medium-high heat. Add artichokes and cook, stirring often, until lightly browned, about 5 minutes. Add zucchini and scallions and cook until zucchini is lightly browned, about 3 minutes. Reduce heat to medium-low, cover, and cook until vegetables are soft, about 10 minutes.

3. Meanwhile, combine bread crumbs, thyme, remaining 3 tbsp. of the oil, and half the parsley in a medium bowl. Season to taste with salt and pepper and set aside. Pick through crabmeat, removing any bits of shell, and set aside.

4. Preheat broiler and set rack about 4" from the heat. When vegetables are soft, increase heat to medium, add crabmeat and remaining parsley, and season to taste with salt and pepper. Cook, stirring gently, until crabmeat is warmed through, about 3 minutes, taking care not to break up crabmeat lumps. Remove from heat and stir in lemon juice. Adjust seasonings.

5. Divide crabmeat between 4 individual gratin dishes. Cover each with a generous handful of the bread crumbs, then broil until browned, 1–2 minutes.

Gamberoni Grigi al Gratin

(Gratinéed Large Gray Shrimp)

SERVES 8

GIGI NACCARI, for years a noted Venetian fishmonger, served us this dish, made by his friend Carla Meneghin, as part of a huge lunch at his home just outside the city.

6 slices stale white bread, crusts removed

¼ cup finely chopped fresh basil

1 clove garlic, peeled and minced

1 tbsp. freshly grated parmigiano-reggiano

3–4 tbsp. extra-virgin olive oil

Salt and freshly ground black pepper

24 large whole (head on) shrimp, legs removed, shells on

½ cup tocai friulano or other dry Friuli white wine

1. Preheat oven to 400°. Tear bread into pieces and put into bowl of food processor fitted with a steel blade, then pulse to coarse crumbs. Transfer to a medium bowl and add basil, garlic, and parmigiano. Toss with oil and season to taste with salt and pepper. Set aside.

2. To butterfly shrimp, make a deep incision with the tip of a sharp knife in the back, just below the head, and slice down to the tail, cutting through the shell and about halfway through the meat. Spread incision open and flatten shrimp slightly with your fingertips.

3. Stuff each shrimp with some of the reserved bread crumbs, then moisten each with about 1 tsp. wine. Arrange shrimp on a baking sheet and bake in upper third of oven for 10 minutes. Switch oven setting to broil, and broil shrimp until bread crumbs are browned, about 5 minutes.

Beyond Pinot Grigio

The region of Friuli, in far northeastern Italy, produces very little wine by Italian standards—only about 2 percent of the country's annual cascade of wine—but what it does produce, especially the white wine, has improved phenomenally in the past 20 years and has found a place on the best wine lists all over the world. Among the cultivars used for white wine is a local variety, tocai—not to be confused with Hungary's tokaji, to which it is not related—which yields a dry, medium-bodied white with a delicate, aromatic flavor that always reminds us of crisp green grapes. Cheaper (and more accessible) than those overoaked Italian chardonnays and usually much more interesting than pinot grigio, tocai friulano is one of our favorite seafood wines.

Ink Spot

I n the aquatic world, cuttlefish ink may be the defense mechanism of a cephalopod, but in the kitchen, it adopts a new role: the ink (along with that of the squid, which tends to be somewhat lighter in both color and flavor) has long been the source of the dramatic black color characteristic of many of Italy's regional fish, pasta, and rice dishes—especially in the Veneto, Le Marche, and Sicily. Culinary bonus: cuttlefish ink imparts a wonderfully aromatic, almost (and ironically) earthy flavor to the foods it colors.

Seppie in Umido col Nero di Seppia

(Cuttlefish Stewed in Its Ink)

SERVES 6–8

CUTTLEFISH (*Sepia officinalis*) is difficult to find fresh in the United States, but frozen cuttlefish of more than acceptable quality is available. Unfortunately, it's usually sold cleaned, with the ink sacs removed, so if you use it, you may need to buy cuttlefish, or squid, ink separately.

3 lbs. whole fresh or frozen cuttlefish
4 tbsp. extra-virgin olive oil
1 tbsp. butter
1 medium white onion, peeled, halved, and very thinly sliced
½ cup tocai friulano or other dry Friuli white wine
2 tbsp. tomato paste
1 bunch Italian parsley, trimmed and chopped
Salt and freshly ground black pepper

1. Wash cuttlefish under cold running water (defrost first if necessary). Separate heads from bodies with a sharp knife, then remove tentacles and set aside, discarding the eyes and beaks with the hard parts around them. Pull out hard "bone" from bodies and discard. Cut bodies lengthwise to open, being careful not to pierce the small, silvery ink sacs. Detach sacs and set aside. Remove and discard entrails. Peel off thin outer skin under cold running water, if you like. Slice cuttlefish and tentacles into medium-size pieces. Rinse under cold water and set aside to drain.

2. Heat oil and butter in a large pan with lid over medium heat. Add onions and cook, stirring often, until soft, about 10 minutes. Add cuttlefish and reserved tentacles and cook until heated through, then add wine and cook until alcohol has evaporated, 3–5 minutes.

3. Mix together tomato paste and 1 cup water in a small bowl, then add to cuttlefish along with ink sacs (or 2–3 tbsp. cuttlefish ink) and half of the chopped parsley. Stir to mix, pressing on ink sacs (if using) with the back of a wooden spoon to break the skins and release the ink. (Don't worry if some sacs have already broken, losing some of their liquid and leaving a thick ink paste behind.) Reduce heat to medium-low and season to taste with salt and pepper. Cover and cook, stirring occasionally, until cuttlefish is very tender, 40–60 minutes. Uncover pan for the last 10 minutes of cooking to reduce and thicken sauce slightly. Sprinkle with remaining chopped parsley and serve with polenta (see recipe, page 150), if you like.

Baccalà Mantecato

(Creamed Stockfish)

SERVES 8

STOCKFISH, the heart of this Venetian classic, can be a daunting ingredient, taking more time and trouble to prepare than what the rest of Italy calls *baccalà* (which is salt cod)—but the results can be nothing less than addictive.

1 1½–2-lb. dried
  stockfish
3 anchovy filets, chopped
1–2 cloves garlic, peeled
  and minced to a paste
Sunflower oil
Salt

1. Place stockfish in a large bowl or pot and cover with cold water, then place in refrigerator for 4–5 days, tightly covered (to minimize odor), changing water at least 3 times a day and more often if possible, gently bending or flexing fish with your hands each time (to hasten water absorption) until fish is rehydrated and soft.

2. Bring a large pot of water to a boil over high heat. Drain stockfish and cook until flesh is just tender and flakes easily, 8–10 minutes. Drain, reserving 1 cup of the cooking water.

3. While fish is still warm, remove and discard bones, reserving skin and stomach membrane (these help give the finished dish its creamy texture). Tear flesh, skin, and membrane into small pieces and put into a sturdy bowl or the bowl of a standing mixer fitted with a paddle. Add anchovies and garlic.

4. Beat fish vigorously with a wooden spoon or beat on medium-low speed with mixer, while slowly drizzling in just enough oil (about ½ cup) to make the mixture light and creamy, about 30 minutes. Beat in a little reserved cooking water if baccalà is too dry. Season to taste with salt. Serve garnished with chopped fresh Italian parsley and grilled polenta (see recipe, page 150), if you like.

Cod and Man in the Mediterranean

Though fished far away, in the North Atlantic, cod (*Gadus morhua*)—not fresh but air-dried or salted—has for centuries been the definitive food fish of the Mediterranean and was long one of the region's principal items of trade as well, imported from northern Europe in exchange for olive oil, wine, and other products of warmer climes. Air-dried cod, or stockfish—*stoccafisso* in Italian—has been on the menu in the Veneto, Liguria, Sicily, and Campania, among other places, since the 16th century. Salt cod, which is *baccalà* everywhere in Italy except the Veneto, arrived only slightly later. Something

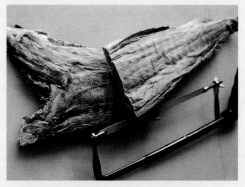

like 90 percent of the world's stockfish is produced in Norway and typically air-dried on wooden frames in the cold, dry Lofoten Islands (most of the rest comes from Iceland); Italy buys about 60 percent of the Norwegian production. (The best quality stockfish is called in Italy *ragno*, which some scholars believe derives from the Norwegian name Ragnor, perhaps an early exporter of the fish.) Stockfish is literally stick hard—both its English and its Italian names derive from the Middle Dutch *stocvisch*, stickfish—to the point that if you buy it whole (it is also sold in pieces) and need to cut it to fit it into a vessel for soaking, you must use a hacksaw. Some cooks even bang it gently with a mallet before soaking to tenderize its fiber.

Vino Bars

What would we do without the *bacari*, the wine bars of Venice, with their honest vino and succulent cicchetti? These are Venetian tapas, if you will, designed to help hungry locals make it through that endless stretch from breakfast to lunch, fill the gaping hole from then till dinner, and salve the ensuing emptiness until bedtime. We're sucked in by the abundant array in the windows of places like Osteria da Alberto (facing page, top left and bottom right)—marinated scampi, the tiny octopi called folpetti, sarde in saor, radicchio salad. Fresh supplies arrive from the kitchen every few minutes: now it's mozzarella with anchovies, tuna croquettes, fried olives…. Then there's Osteria do Mori (top right and bottom left), near the Rialto market, one of the oldest bacari. We walk in out of the crisp morning air and thank God for the tramezzini (little triangular sandwiches), warm musetto (pig-muzzle sausage) with cranberry beans, and hearty merlot from Friuli. After all, it *is* 8:30 A.M.

Sarde in Saor
(Marinated Sardines)

SERVES 6

THE RECIPE for this centuries-old dish comes from the excellent Fiaschetteria Toscana, near Venice's famed Rialto Bridge—a very Venetian establishment, despite its name.

2 lbs. medium-size fresh sardines, cleaned and scaled
Vegetable oil
1 cup flour
Salt
3 large white onions, peeled, halved, and very thinly sliced
¼ cup extra-virgin olive oil
2 shallots, peeled and minced
¾ cup raisins
¾ cup pine nuts
¾ cup white wine vinegar

1. Rinse sardines and cut off heads and tails. Using a sharp knife, slice each fish open so that it lies flat, skin side down. Remove and discard bones using the tip of the knife or by running your index finger between backbone and flesh. Rinse sardines again and pat dry.

2. Pour vegetable oil into a large skillet to a depth of ½" and heat over high heat. Dredge sardines in flour and fry until lightly golden, about 15 seconds per side. Drain on paper towels. Season to taste with salt.

3. Bring a medium pot of water to a boil. Add onions, blanch for 10 seconds, then drain. Heat olive oil in a large skillet over medium-low heat. Add onions and shallots and cook, stirring often, until very soft, 20–30 minutes. Add raisins, pine nuts, and 6 tbsp. of the vinegar and season to taste with salt. Reduce heat to low and cook, stirring often, until vinegar has been absorbed, about 20 minutes. Set aside to cool.

4. Layer onions and sardines in a ceramic dish, beginning and ending with onions. Sprinkle remaining 6 tbsp. of vinegar between layers. Cover and set aside for 2–3 days in a cool place—not in refrigerator. Serve at room temperature, with room-temperature fried polenta (see recipe, page 150), if you like.

Fritto Misto

(Mixed Fried Seafood and Vegetables)

SERVES 4

AL COVO, one of our favorite Venetian restaurants, shared with us its recipe for this popular Adriatic specialty. We think its fritto misto just might be the best one in Venice.

¼ cup cornstarch
1½ cups all-purpose flour
1½ cups cake flour
Sparkling mineral water
Salt and freshly ground
    black pepper
¼ lb. whole small shrimp,
    peeled
¼ lb. sole filet, cut into
    2" × 3" pieces
¼ lb. squid, cleaned (see
    sidebar, page 121) and
    cut into rings and
    tentacle pieces
¼ lb. bay scallops
Peanut oil
Grapeseed oil
¼ lb. green beans,
    trimmed
1 medium red bell pepper,
    stemmed, cored, seeded,
    and sliced into strips
1 medium zucchini,
    trimmed and thinly
    sliced

1. Mix cornstarch and ⅓ cup of each flour with 1 cup of sparkling water until it reaches the consistency of a thin batter, adding more water if necessary. Season to taste with salt and pepper, cover, and refrigerate for 2 hours.

2. Chill shrimp, sole, and squid together in one bowl of ice water and scallops in another.

3. Preheat oven to lowest setting. Pour equal amounts of peanut and grapeseed oil into a large, heavy skillet to a depth of 2". Heat over high heat until hot but not smoking, about 375° on a candy thermometer. Mix together remaining all-purpose and cake flours. Drain shrimp, sole, and squid and dredge in flour. Fry in batches until seafood is crisp, about 2 minutes. Drain on paper towels, then transfer to oven to keep warm. Drain scallops, dredge in flour, and fry until crisp, about 1½ minutes. Drain and transfer to oven.

4. Dip vegetables into reserved batter and fry in batches until crisp, about 2 minutes. Combine vegetables and seafood on a platter, sprinkle with salt, and serve with lemon wedges, if you like.

Little Italy

Back in the 1970s, our friend Bill Stern, who had spent a fair amount of time eating in Italy, declared in print that there were no Italian restaurants in America. His statement provoked a storm of demurs, of course—but his well-taken point was that the food you got in those (nonexistent) Italian restaurants in America mostly had very little to do with what Italians ate in their homeland. Instead of garlic-rubbed grilled bread, thin-sliced cured pork products, tangles of bitter greens, lightly (simply) sauced pastas, plain grilled meats, and roasted fish or fowl, Italian restaurants here were serving caesar salad (invented in that rustic Italian hill town Tijuana), shrimp swimming in butter sauce, spaghetti with handball-size spheres of ground meat and oceans of tomato sauce, veal smothered in chewy melted cheese.... Now, we eat broccoletti and porcini, radicchio and arugula, aceto balsamico and bruschetta; we know the cuisines of Puglia, Liguria, the monzùs of Sicily; our cities are as well equipped with Tuscan trattorias as they are with Starbucks. We love it all. But we also—*pace* Mr. Stern— still like an occasional "shrimp scampi" or veal parmigiana. They may not be real Italian food, but they're *our* Italian food.

Shrimp Scampi
(Scampi-Style Shrimp)

SERVES 6

PURISTS complain that this Italian-American specialty (our recipe comes from the legendary Rao's in Manhattan) has a contradictory name: shrimp and scampi (Adriatic crayfish) are two different things. That's quite true, but we think the name's fine: it just means "shrimp cooked scampi style".

2 lbs. large shrimp, peeled, deveined, and butterflied
1 cup flour
1 cup extra-virgin olive oil
1½ cups dry white wine
1 tbsp. Worcestershire sauce or more to taste
5 cloves garlic, peeled and minced
Juice of 1½ lemons (about 5 tbsp.)
½ cup chicken stock
8 tbsp. butter, cut into small pieces
Salt and freshly ground black pepper
2 tbsp. minced fresh Italian parsley

1. Dredge shrimp in flour and set aside. Meanwhile, heat oil in a large skillet over high heat. Working in batches, sauté shrimp until just golden, about 2 minutes. Transfer to a paper-towel-lined plate. Repeat process until all shrimp have been sautéed.

2. Drain and discard excess oil from pan, add wine, Worcestershire sauce, garlic, lemon juice, and stock to pan. Cook over high heat until liquid is reduced by half, about 5 minutes. Whisk in butter and season to taste with salt and pepper. Reduce heat to medium and add shrimp to reheat, tossing to coat well with sauce, for about 1 minute. Sprinkle with parsley just before serving.

Cacciucco

(Livorno-Style Fish Stew)

SERVES 6

EVEN WITH ITALY'S many coastal regions—15 out of 20—fresh fish hasn't always had a preeminent spot at the table. This stew was once considered only a poor man's dish.

1 lb. manila or littleneck clams
Salt
½ lb. medium shrimp, unpeeled
1 2-lb. whole small fish (for instance, red snapper or striped bass), cleaned and scaled
1 lb. halibut filets
⅓ cup extra-virgin olive oil
4 cloves garlic, peeled
¼ tsp. red pepper flakes
1 small yellow onion, peeled and minced
1 small carrot, peeled, trimmed, and minced
1 rib celery, trimmed and minced
6 sprigs fresh Italian parsley, finely chopped
1 cup dry red wine
1 28-oz. can peeled Italian tomatoes, drained and coarsely chopped
Freshly ground black pepper
1 lb. small squid, cleaned (see sidebar, page 121) and cut into pieces
1 lb. mussels, scrubbed and debearded
6 slices crusty Italian bread, toasted

1. Soak clams in a large bowl of salted water to purge them of any sand and grit. Meanwhile, clean shrimp, removing any dark veins and pulling off and reserving shells (leave tails on).

2. Cut off and reserve head, tail, and fins from whole fish. Cut fish crosswise, through the backbone, into four 1"-thick steaks and set aside. Cut halibut filets into pieces about 1" x 3" x 1" and set aside. Drain and rinse clams well and set aside.

3. Heat oil in a large saucepan over medium-high heat; add 3 of the garlic cloves and sauté until golden, 1–2 minutes, then remove and discard garlic. Add red pepper flakes, onion, carrot, celery, and parsley and sauté until soft, about 3 minutes. Add wine and cook until it has almost evaporated, then add tomatoes. Season to taste with salt and pepper and bring to a boil, then reduce heat to medium-low and simmer for about 10 minutes.

4. Add reserved shrimp shells and fish head, tail, and fins. Add 4 cups of hot water, increase heat to high, bring to a boil, then reduce heat to medium-low and simmer for 20 minutes. Remove from heat and strain stock through a coarse sieve into a large wide pot, discarding solids.

5. Add fish steaks and filets to the stock, then add squid and bring to a simmer over medium-high heat. (Stock should just cover fish; add a little hot water if necessary.) Add mussels, clams, and shrimp, cover, and simmer until mussels and clams open and shrimp turn pink, about 5 minutes. To serve, rub toasted bread with remaining clove of garlic and place 1 slice in each of 6 wide soup plates, then ladle cacciucco over bread.

The Tuscan Riviera

Most people are familiar with Tuscany's countryside, but few associate the lush region with water. In fact, Tuscany's western side consists of a coastline with exclusive seaside resorts that run from Forte dei Marmi to Porto Ercole. And since the 16th century, the city of Livorno has been one of the largest commercial ports in the Mediterranean. While there are many species of fish available at the market, Tuscans pride themselves on using local varieties. The gastronomic value of fish is illustrated by such regional dishes as cacciucco—made with fish including moscardini (small octopus) and spannocchie (mantis shrimp)—and triglie alla Livornese (red mullet cooked with tomatoes).

POULTRY AND RABBIT

"BY LAW, the *frasche* of Friuli may serve

only foods produced on the premises.

Named for the branch (*frasca*) tradition-

ally hung in front of farms with new wine

to sell, these establishments offer sim-

ple fare—homemade cheese and salami,

hearty gnocchi, roasted fowl, polenta—

often with wine from the property, all of

it usually served under something deli-

ciously flowering or budding." —EUGENIA BONE

Pollo alla Diavola

(Chicken "Devil Style")

SERVES 4–8

TRUE POLLO alla diavola is liberally seasoned with red pepper flakes. Claudio Ciocca leaves them out of his version at Il Fico Vecchio, in the hills near Rome; his customers have timid palates, he says. Feel free to add them if you like.

2 3½-lb. chickens
3 lemons
¾ cup extra-virgin
    olive oil
Salt and freshly ground
    black pepper

1. Using a sharp knife or kitchen shears, remove chicken backs by cutting along both sides of the backbone. Discard backbones or save for making stock. Rinse birds and pat dry with paper towels. Place butterflied chickens on a cutting board skin side up and roll birds with a rolling pin, leaning heavily on the pin to flatten them.

2. Place chicken in a wide, deep dish. Squeeze the juice from 2 of the lemons over birds, add ½ cup of the oil, and season to taste with salt and lots of pepper. Set aside to let marinate for 30–60 minutes.

3. Meanwhile, preheat grill. Squeeze juice from the remaining lemon into a small bowl, whisk in the remaining ¼ cup oil, and season to taste with salt and lots of pepper, then set aside. Remove chickens from marinade, discarding marinade. Grill birds over medium-hot coals, basting occasionally with the reserved lemon and oil, until skin is well browned on both sides and thigh juices run clear when pricked with a fork, about 50 minutes. Set chickens aside to let rest for 10 minutes, then cut into quarters.

Hill Country Fare

One of our favorite restaurants in the Castelli Romani, as the hills a few miles southeast of the city are known, is Il Fico Vecchio in Grottaferrata. The proprietor is Claudio Ciocca (above), a handsome former member of the Fellini stock company with a snowy white ponytail and a welcoming smile. The place has grown casually prosperous over the years; its once simple tables are now set with overlapping white linens and hotel silver. Ciocca's food is still the modest, flawless Roman country fare we remember from decades ago—from fresh ricotta, broccoli salad, and bruschetta to pastas like the earthy rigatoni alla pagliata (a uniquely and dauntingly Roman specialty of tube-shaped pasta tossed with similar-looking lengths of the intestines of suckling lambs) to roasted meats and grilled chicken—followed, of course, by fresh fruit and good cheese.

Important Chicken

In 21st-century America, chicken is a commonplace, a fast-food staple, an all-purpose (and inoffensive) form of protein that comes in many forms—even as sausage or "burger" meat. In the Italian countryside of an earlier time, in contrast, this barnyard bird was a creature of real significance—far too valuable (for its eggs) to end up on the table on an average night. Even in relatively prosperous households, chicken might be on the menu only once a week, usually for Sunday supper. Among poorer families, a fowl might be slaughtered only a few times a year, for consumption on Christmas or other big holidays or as the centerpiece at wedding or anniversary banquets. That's probably why there are comparatively few chicken recipes in Italian cuisine. When chicken was cooked, it was most often roasted whole, the leftover bones used to flavor soups and the scraps ground up for pasta sauce or pasta filling.

Pollo alla Cacciatora
(Hunter's Wife's Chicken)

SERVES 4

AMERICANS MAY know this dish as *cacciatore* (hunter's style), but it's really cacciator*a*, named in honor of the hunter's wife—who, in parts of northern Italy, traditionally cooked it on the eve of the hunt as fuel for the chase.

¼ cup extra-virgin olive oil
2 medium yellow onions, peeled and chopped
2 cloves garlic, peeled and minced
1 3-lb. chicken, cut into 8 pieces
1 cup dry white wine
1 28-oz. can peeled whole Italian plum tomatoes, chopped, juice reserved
1 bay leaf
1 tsp. minced fresh rosemary leaves
¼ cup minced fresh Italian parsley
Salt and freshly ground black pepper
1 cup strong chicken stock

1. Heat oil in a large pan over medium-high heat. Add onions and cook, stirring occasionally, until soft, about 10 minutes. Add garlic and cook, continuing to stir, for about 2 minutes more. Push onions to sides of pan, then add chicken and fry, turning pieces several times to brown evenly, about 4 minutes per side.

2. Add wine and cook until it evaporates, about 5 minutes. Add tomatoes, with their juice, to chicken. Stir in bay leaf, rosemary, and parsley (reserving 1 tbsp. or so for garnish) and season to taste with salt and pepper. Reduce heat to low, partially cover, and simmer, adding chicken stock gradually as tomato juice evaporates, for 45 minutes. Remove bay leaf and garnish with reserved parsley. Serve with steamed potatoes or white rice.

Quaglia con Salsa di Fichi

(Quail with Fig Sauce)

SERVES 4

ADAPTING A FAVORITE old family recipe for wild boar with figs and raisins, Ed Giobbi—an artist, author, and Arthur Avenue regular whose ancestors come from Italy's Le Marche region—created this savory quail dish.

1 clove garlic, peeled and minced

3 tbsp. extra-virgin olive oil

1 tbsp. finely chopped fresh rosemary

2 tsp. finely chopped fresh sage leaves

8 quail, butterflied

6 dried figs, coarsely chopped

1 cup marsala

2 oz. pancetta, coarsely chopped

3 shallots, peeled and minced

1 cup chicken stock

1. Mix together garlic, oil, half the rosemary, and half the sage in a large, shallow bowl. Add quail, mix well, and set aside for 30 minutes. Place chopped figs and marsala in a small bowl and set aside until figs begin to soften, about 30 minutes.

2. Heat a large skillet over medium heat. Add pancetta and cook until fat is rendered and pancetta is crisp, about 8 minutes. Remove pancetta from skillet and set aside. Add half the quail (with marinade) to skillet and brown for about 6 minutes on each side, then remove and set aside; brown remaining quail and set aside.

3. Add shallots to skillet and cook until soft, about 10 minutes. Increase heat to medium-high, add figs and marsala, and cook until pan is almost dry, 5–10 minutes more. Add stock, bring to a simmer, then reduce heat to medium and cook until figs are very soft, 10–15 minutes. Add pancetta and remaining herbs to sauce. Warm quail in sauce, in batches, for about 5 minutes per batch. Transfer quail and sauce to a large platter. Serve with polenta and garnish with fresh figs, if you like.

Arthur Avenue

Self-trained cook Ed Giobbi helped to emancipate Italian food in America from the tired old spaghetti-and-meatball clichés with his *Italian Family Cooking* (Random House, 1971). Connecticut born but with roots in the region of Le Marche, Giobbi is immensely proud of his Italian heritage. For a slice of the old country, he makes weekly trips to Arthur Avenue (scenes on facing page), the great Italian market street in the Bronx, just northeast of Manhattan. Ethnic pride runs deep in this community of 10,000 Italian-Americans. Indeed, the main drag contains what is perhaps the greatest concentration of authentic Italian food merchants east of the Mississippi. More than 200 Italian businesses—most of them food related—are packed into seven Bronx blocks. "I will never forget," says writer Eugenia Bone (above, in an Arthur Avenue shop), who is Giobbi's daughter, "the first time my father came home from a shopping spree on Arthur Avenue, about a decade ago. It was as if he'd witnessed a miracle. As he unpacked the bargain-priced treasures he'd collected—a plump pullet, frilly puntarella, fresh bread with airholes the size of a child's fist—his face was almost beatific."

Game Birds

T here's more than one way to catch a game bird," writes SAVEUR editor Colman Andrews. "I remember seeing a little painting in the Palais des Papes in Avignon depicting servants brushing glue on tree branches to ensnare hapless winged creatures. And when I visited the excellent Volpe Pasini winery, built on the grounds of the old summer estate of the patriarchs of Aquileia, just northwest of Cividale del Friuli in prime Friuli wine country, I was shown the remains of an old *uccellanda*. The word can mean a kind of marsh (habitat of birds galore) but in this case referred to an elaborate oversize bird trap. The uccellanda consisted of a circle of trees and wooden posts, about 40 feet in diameter, with a birdcage on a pillar exactly in the center. In the old days, my hosts told me, a chattering bird of some kind would be shut into the cage and a huge net would be lifted up to tree level, completely covering the top of the circle but leaving the sides free. Many birds would fly in to join the chatterer, and the net would be dropped. 'Hunters' would then wade in, pulling birds through the net, tossing inedible species back into the air and breaking the necks of the tasty ones. Fortunately for the birds and for our sensibilities, the practice is now long extinct."

Faraona Rustît

(Roast Stuffed Guinea Hen)

SERVES 2

RELATED TO PHEASANT, guinea hen is underused in the United States. The recipe for this classic country dish comes from Ennio Furlan, the former cook at Agriturismo de Carvalho in Manzano, about ten miles east of Udine.

FOR STUFFING:
4 oz. ground pork
2 oz. ground beef
1 egg
Generous pinch ground
    nutmeg
5–6 sprigs fresh Italian
    parsley, finely chopped
Salt and freshly ground
    black pepper

FOR GUINEA HEN:
1 2½-lb. guinea hen
Salt and freshly ground
    black pepper
Extra-virgin olive oil
1 carrot, peeled and
    trimmed
1 rib celery, trimmed
2 cloves garlic, peeled
1 medium yellow onion,
    peeled and chopped
2 sprigs fresh rosemary
6–8 sprigs fresh thyme
1 cup dry white wine
2 tbsp. flour
1 cup chicken stock

1. For stuffing, mix together pork, beef, egg, nutmeg, and parsley and season to taste with salt and pepper. Form into a fat sausage shape, then wrap tightly in plastic to keep its shape while cooking.

2. For guinea hen, preheat oven to 450°. Wash guinea hen and dry with paper towels, then season inside and out with salt and pepper. Place wrapped stuffing into cavity and truss bird.

3. Lightly oil a medium shallow roasting pan and arrange carrot, celery, garlic, onions, rosemary, and half the thyme in the center. Put guinea hen on top of vegetables and roast until bird is browned, 15–20 minutes. Reduce heat to 375°, pour wine into pan around bird, and continue roasting for about 45 minutes.

4. Transfer bird to a platter. Untruss, then remove stuffing from cavity, unwrap, and cut into slices about ¾" thick; arrange on platter and set aside.

5. Remove and discard vegetables, then stir flour into pan drippings and add remaining thyme sprigs. Cook on top of the stove over medium heat for 2–3 minutes, then add stock. Increase heat to high and reduce for 3 minutes. Serve guinea hen and sausage stuffing with sauce, and with polenta (see page 150), if you like.

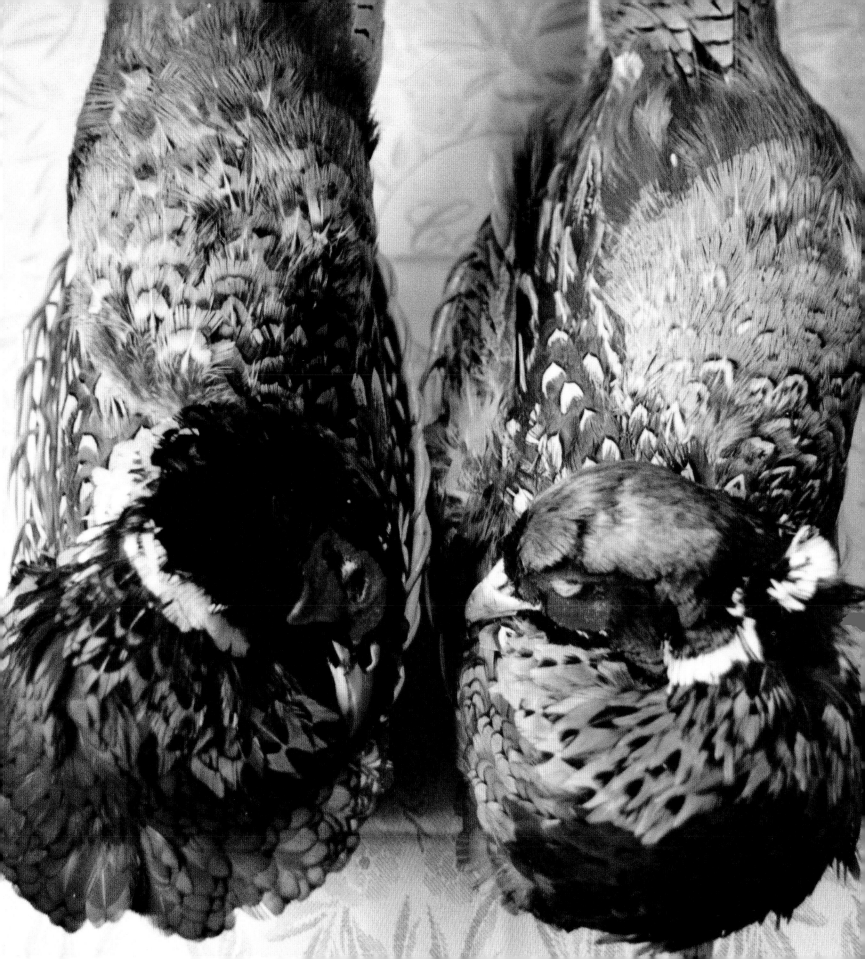

Italy or Not

For nearly 400 years, the Adriatic peninsula of Istria was ruled by the Venetian empire. In our own century, it has belonged to Hapsburg Austria, to Italy, and, from 1945 to 1991, to Yugoslavia. Today it is part of Croatia. As a result of Istria's varied past, its cuisine is fascinating—an amalgam of Austro-Hungarian, Italian, and Slavic traditions, including hearty game dishes, fresh seafood, dense vegetable soups, unusual pastas (such as fuzi, shaped like little open envelopes), and rich desserts like strudel and palacinke (sweet Slavic crêpes). The capital of Istria, Pula, today a city of about 80,000, is a mix of splendid Roman ruins, solidly elegant turn-of-the-century Hapsburg buildings, and grim Communist-era concrete monoliths. In the crowded center of town, the market has changed little in the past 40 years: the vendors still stand behind produce heaped on long, waist-high stone tables, shaded by chestnut trees, whose tender new leaves droop like handkerchiefs.

Crepnia di Coniglio e Patate

(Baked Rabbit and Potatoes)

SERVES 6

IN ISTRIA, the term *crepnia* applies both to a shallow steel pan with a high lid and to the food—usually some combination of meat and vegetables—cooked in the pan. This recipe comes from Istrian-born New York restaurateur Lidia Bastianich, left (with cousin Milena Pavichievaz).

2 3-lb. whole rabbits
18 new potatoes
2 medium yellow onions, peeled and quartered
10 cloves garlic, peeled
1 cup dry white wine
6 tbsp. extra-virgin olive oil
Leaves from 1 medium branch fresh sage
1 medium branch fresh rosemary, broken into thirds
2 tbsp. red wine vinegar
Coarse sea salt
Freshly ground black pepper

1. Build a hot fire in a pizza oven or outdoor grill using wood and/or hardwood charcoal.

2. Meanwhile, lay each rabbit on its back and, using a sharp knife, cut off hind legs at the joint near the backbone. Cut under shoulder blades to remove forelegs from rib cage. Trim off rib cage on either side of loin and discard, then trim neck and tail ends of loin and discard. Cut loin crosswise (through backbone) into 2–3 pieces.

3. Combine rabbit, potatoes, onions, garlic, wine, oil, sage, rosemary, and vinegar in a large bowl. Season to taste with salt and pepper and mix well. Transfer to a crepnia or a heavy, two-handled, flat-bottomed wok. Cover crepnia with lid, or cover wok with a large, flat-bottomed stainless-steel bowl turned upside down (bowl should be same circumference as wok).

4. When fire has died down, shovel embers off to sides of pizza oven or grill. Place crepnia in pizza oven or nestle it down in grill. Shovel embers on top and around crepnia, then close lid of grill, if using. Cook until rabbit and potatoes are tender and brown and juices have thickened and caramelized, about 45 minutes. Remove from oven or grill and set aside to let rest, still covered, for about 10 minutes before serving.

Italy, Missouri

I n the close-knit, lively St. Louis neighborhood known as the Hill," writes St. Louis native Bill Sertl, "food is the tie that binds and satisfies. A one-square-mile Italian stronghold just west of Downtown and the Gateway Arch, the Hill—where about 75 percent of the residents are still of Italian ancestry (the first Italians arrived here in the 1880s)—is home to shops like Volpi Italian Foods, producer of some of the best salami and prosciutto in America. Above the meat cases are vintage photographs, one of a delivery truck in the '40s and another of company founder John Volpi. Pudgy sausages hang from the rafters, and the countertops are crammed with impulse buys— Italian licorice, chocolate-covered coffee beans, packages of dried porcini. Overseeing the whole operation is Armando Pasetti, an outgoing Lombard who is John Volpi's nephew and who took over the company after his uncle's death in 1957. 'I learned by watching my uncle,' Pasetti says. About his braised rabbit, the always modest Volpi adds, 'It's nothing. A little garlic, a little olive oil.'"

Armando's Braised Rabbit

SERVES 6–8

ARMANDO PASETTI of Volpi Italian Foods in St. Louis created this dish years ago and often serves it with soft polenta; when he does, Pasetti says, he makes extra sauce.

2 3-lb. whole rabbits
½ oz. dried porcini
1 small yellow onion,
   peeled and
   finely chopped
1 clove garlic, peeled and
   minced
2 tbsp. chopped fresh
   Italian parsley
½ tsp. dried oregano
2 whole cloves
¼ cup extra-virgin
   olive oil
¼ cup balsamic vinegar
1 bay leaf
Salt and freshly ground
   black pepper
1 cup dry white wine
1 cup chicken stock

1. Lay each rabbit on its back. Using a sharp knife, cut off hind legs at the joint near the backbone. Cut under shoulder blades to remove forelegs from rib cage. Trim off rib cage on either side of loin and discard, then trim neck and tail ends of loin and discard. Cut loin crosswise (through backbone) into 2–3 pieces.

2. Put porcini into a small bowl, cover with warm water, and soak until soft, about 30 minutes. Lift porcini from soaking liquid with a fork and finely chop; discard liquid. Transfer porcini to a large bowl and add onions, garlic, parsley, oregano, cloves, oil, vinegar, and bay leaf and season to taste with salt and pepper. Mix well. Add rabbit pieces and rub with marinade. Cover with plastic wrap and refrigerate overnight.

3. Heat a large skillet over medium-high heat, add rabbit with marinade, and sauté until meat is brown on all sides, 5–10 minutes. Add wine and cook until alcohol has evaporated, about 2 minutes. Stir with a wooden spoon, scraping any brown bits from bottom of pan.

4. Add chicken stock and bring to a simmer. Reduce heat to medium-low, cover, and cook, turning pieces occasionally, until rabbit is just cooked through and tender but not dry, 30–40 minutes. Uncover and continue cooking until sauce thickens slightly, 5–10 minutes. Remove bay leaf, adjust seasonings, and serve with polenta (see recipe, page 150), if you like.

Fritto di Coniglio e Fiori di Zucca

(Fried Rabbit and Squash Blossoms)

SERVES 4

TUSCANS like frying food as much as they like grilling and roasting it, as we first discovered years ago at I Ricchi, in the hills above Florence, where we learned how to make this dish.

¼ cup cornstarch
1 cup all-purpose flour
⅓ cup cake flour
Sparkling water
Salt and freshly ground
    black pepper
1 3-lb. rabbit, cut into
    10 pieces
4 eggs, lightly beaten
Extra-virgin olive oil
2 medium red onions,
    peeled, cut into
    ½"-thick slices, and
    separated into rings
12 blossoms of zucchini
    or other squash,
    stamens removed

1. Mix cornstarch and ⅓ cup of each flour with 1 cup of the sparkling water until mixture reaches the consistency of a thin batter, adding more water if necessary. Season to taste with salt and pepper, cover, and refrigerate for 2 hours.

2. Generously season rabbit with salt and pepper, then dip rabbit in beaten eggs and shake off excess. Very lightly dust rabbit with flour, shaking off any excess, then dip rabbit into beaten eggs for a second time. Set pieces aside on a baking sheet.

3. Meanwhile, pour oil into a heavy pot to a depth of about 2". Heat over medium-high heat until hot but not smoking, about 375° on a candy thermometer. Fry rabbit in 2 batches, to avoid lowering temperature of oil, until it is tender and deep golden, 8–10 minutes. Lower heat if oil gets too hot.

4. Remove rabbit from oil with tongs or a slotted spoon as it is done and drain on paper towels. Dip onion rings and squash blossoms into reserved batter and fry in batches until golden, about 2 minutes per batch. Remove from oil and drain on paper towels. Season with salt and pepper and serve with rabbit.

In the Oil

The Tuscans—along with the Ligurians and the Venetians—are Italy's masters of the art of frying. The medium of choice, not surprisingly, is olive oil, and although some self-styled experts will tell you to use the cheap stuff for frying and the delicate kind for salad dressing, Tuscans prefer to fry with a mild oil (not necessarily from Tuscany), one that will add flavor to the dish without overpowering it. Also important for superior frying, say Tuscans: measure the temperature of the oil with a candy thermometer to avoid burning the exterior of the food and undercooking the interior. The optimal temperature depends on what you're cooking but should never exceed the smoke point of the oil (375° for olive oil).

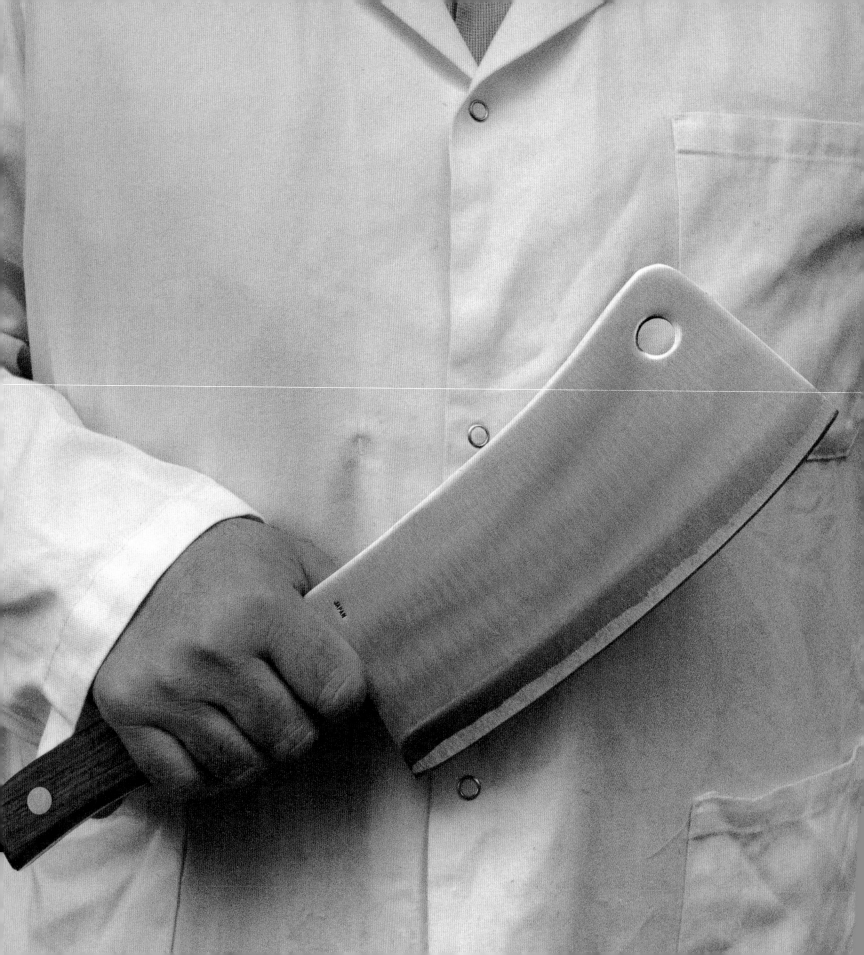

MEATS

"IT IS sometimes said that the Milanese

care only for business and not for the real

pleasures of life. For evidence to the con-

trary, visit Peck, Milan's great food shop,

(top left and bottom right) where Italy's bounty is arrayed—from heads on chickens to straw-wrapped cheese to heaps of white truffles and tons of the finest veal. Sure, the Milanese like to make money; and they know just what to spend it on." —COLMAN ANDREWS

Coscia 'i Maiali Arrustutu

(Sicilian Roast Pork Loin)

SERVES 6

THIS IS one of the local specialties actor and cookbook author Vincent Schiavelli (below) made when he visited Polizzi Generosa, where his Sicilian grandfather once cooked.

Salt
1 3-lb. boneless loin
*   of pork*
1 tbsp. black peppercorns
1 small yellow onion,
*   peeled and finely*
*   chopped*
6 russet potatoes, peeled
*   and chopped into large*
*   pieces*
3 tbsp. extra-virgin
*   olive oil*
1 cup dry white wine

1. Preheat oven to 375°. Generously salt pork loin, then put it on a roasting rack fitted into a medium roasting pan.

2. Wrap peppercorns in a clean kitchen towel, then crush by pressing with the bottom of a heavy skillet or tapping gently with a mallet. (Peppercorns should be cracked, not ground.) Pat cracked pepper on top of pork loin, then add chopped onions, patting them gently into place on top of loin.

3. Put potatoes into a mixing bowl and toss with salt and oil, then add to roasting pan. Roast pork and potatoes for 45 minutes, then add wine. Stir potatoes and cook for an additional 45 minutes, basting occasionally. Remove pan from oven, transfer pork to a cutting board, and allow to rest for 5 minutes before carving. Transfer potatoes to a platter, arrange sliced pork loin over potatoes, and top with any pan juices.

Memorable Generosity

Located about 50 miles east of Palermo, in the Madonie Mountains, Polizzi Generosa is said to have been named Polis Isis—the City of Isis, in honor of the Egyptian goddess Isis—by a Greek cult that worshiped her and lived here in the fourth and fifth centuries B.C. About 1,700 years later, in 1234, the Holy Roman Emperor Frederick II—who was also king of Sicily—visited Polizzi and was so moved by the warm welcome the city extended to him that he decreed it "La Generosa", the generous. As anyone who visits the restaurants or home kitchens of the town today will soon realize, that characterization remains appropriate.

Saltimbocca alla Romana

(Veal Scaloppine with Prosciutto and Sage)

SERVES 4

THIS version of the dish Romans call saltimbocca, or "jump in the mouth" (for its savory appeal), comes from La Buca di Ripetta, a modest trattoria in Rome's historic center.

Rome Again

I got to know Rome in every season in the 1970s," remembers SAVEUR editor Colman Andrews (above left, circa 1972), who recently revisited his old Roman haunts with friends from 30 years ago, Karen and Gianfranco (above center and right). "But my most vivid memories of the city, and especially of eating in the city, are autumnal. In the fall, the light turns thick and golden, and the first roasted chestnut sellers set up their carts on street corners, perfuming the air with savory smoke. Restaurant windows glow with heaps of meaty funghi por-cini, and wild quail and pheasants hang from the ceilings in their faintly iridescent feathered glory, next to still-fragrant bouquets of drying late-summer herbs. We ate all the Roman specialties—bruschetta, fettuccine Alfredo, spaghetti alla puttanesca, abbacchio al forno, saltimbocca...Returning to the city in 1999, I frankly feared that these great old dishes would have disappeared or would now be cloaked in balsamic glaze or white truffle oil, those twin banes of contemporary pseudo-Italian cooking. Happily, though, we found the cooking remarkably unchanged—as befits the Eternal City."

4 pieces thinly sliced prosciutto, cut in half crosswise
1 lb. veal scaloppine, cut into 8 pieces
8 large fresh sage leaves
¼ cup extra-virgin olive oil
¼ cup dry white wine
1 cup brodo di carne (see page 76) or veal, chicken, or beef stock
4 tbsp. butter, in pieces

1. Place 1 slice of prosciutto on top of each slice of veal, center a sage leaf on top of prosciutto, then thread a wooden toothpick through sage, prosciutto, and veal to hold all 3 in place. Set aside.

2. Heat oil in a large skillet over medium heat until hot but not smoking. Add prepared meat to skillet, prosciutto side down, in a single layer (work in batches, if necessary) and sauté until prosciutto is slightly browned and crisp on edges and veal is lighly browned, about 2 minutes. Turn and brown other side for 1 minute. As meat is cooked, transfer to a warm platter.

3. Pour off and discard fat from skillet. Return skillet to medium-high heat, add wine, and cook, scraping browned bits stuck to bottom of skillet, until alcohol has evaporated, about 1 minute. Add stock and accumulated juices from platter and reduce by three-quarters, about 10 minutes, then whisk in butter. Return saltimbocca to skillet just long enough to heat through, then transfer to a serving platter, prosciutto side up, and spoon sauce over the top. Remove toothpicks before serving.

Costoletta alla Milanese

(*Milanese-Style Veal Cutlet*)

SERVES 2

THIS RECIPE comes from Don Lisander in Milan, famous for its real Milanese cooking. Leaving the bone attached when pounding out the veal is the Milanese style, as is serving a little salad of chopped tomatoes on the side.

1 1-lb. veal rib chop
Salt and freshly ground
 black pepper
1 egg, lightly beaten
1 cup fine bread crumbs
Extra-virgin olive oil

1. For presentation, clean rib bone by cutting off all meat and fat, then trim fat from the chop meat. Slice chop crosswise as though butterflying it, but continue cutting meat into 2 chops, one with a bone and one without. Season meat on both sides with salt and pepper. Place a sheet of wax paper or plastic wrap on top of each piece of meat, then use a meat pounder, working from the center with outward strokes, to pound meat flat.

2. Pour beaten egg onto a plate and put bread crumbs onto another. Dip one chop at a time into egg, coating it evenly on each side, then dredge in bread crumbs.

3. Preheat oven to 300°. Heat 2 tbsp. of oil in a large nonstick skillet over medium-high heat. Fry chop on the bone, turning only once, until bread crumbs are golden brown, about 2 minutes on each side.

4. Place browned chop on an ovenproof plate, cover lightly with aluminum foil, and set aside. Wipe out pan with paper towel and heat 2 tbsp. of oil over medium-high heat. Fry remaining chop as you did the first, add it to the same ovenproof plate, then transfer plate to oven to finish cooking, 4–6 minutes. Garnish with chopped tomato salad, if you like.

Getting to Know You

N amed for the fierce Longobards who once pillaged the Italian peninsula, Lombardy is famous today for its lakes, its fertile farmland, and its capital: Milan—the business and manufacturing hub of Italy. Compared with Rome or even industrial Turin, Milan is not an immediately accessible, or likable, city. It's congested, confusing, cold... But it's also, once you start to get to know your way around, a vibrant, stylish, elegant, art-filled (e.g., *The Last Supper*) metropolis, well worth wandering around in. Gaze in awe at Milan's magnificent spun-sugar Duomo, or cathedral; sip coffee in the Italian-Victorian Galleria Vittorio Emanuele (above); hear *Tosca* at La Scala; window-shop at Armani or Peck. Let Milan get to know you, too.

It Matters How You Slice It

Scaloppine—thinly sliced scallops or flat pieces of meat (usually veal)—are used in many classic Italian dishes, including saltimbocca (see page 214), scaloppine di vitello al limone, and involtini (literally, "little parcels") of every kind. Scaloppine are more than just veal thinly sliced, however; they're veal thinly sliced a certain way. To end up with tender meat, ask your butcher to cut your scaloppine from the upper part of the hind leg of veal, always cutting *across* the grain of the meat. Then pound the veal slices with a meat pounder, working from the center with outward strokes. If you are using scaloppine for involtini, be sure that there are no holes or tears in the meat so that the filling doesn't leak out.

Involtini alla Benedettina

(Sicilian Veal Rolls)

SERVES 4

THE FIRST Tornabene ancestor acquired a Benedictine abbey in the Sicilian hamlet of Gangivecchio in 1856. Today, the Tornabenes cook dishes like this at their restaurant there.

FOR FILLING:
1 cup fresh bread crumbs
1 small yellow onion,
    peeled and finely
    chopped
1 cup packed grated
    mozzarella cheese
1 egg
Salt and freshly ground
    black pepper

FOR INVOLTINI:
18 2-oz. pieces veal
    scaloppine
Salt and freshly ground
    pepper
6 thin slices boiled ham,
    cut lengthwise into 18
    1½"-wide strips
Extra-virgin olive oil
1 small yellow onion,
    peeled and finely
    chopped
2 heaping tbsp. tomato
    paste
1 small sprig fresh
    rosemary
Flour

1. For filling, put bread crumbs into a mixing bowl and sprinkle with ¼ cup water. Set aside for a few minutes, then squeeze out excess water and return bread crumbs to bowl. Add onion, mozzarella, and egg and mix together. Season to taste with salt and pepper and set aside.

2. For involtini, lay out scaloppine on a clean surface and season to taste with salt and pepper. Put a piece of ham at the widest end of each scaloppina. Place a rounded tbsp. of the filling about an inch from the wide edge of each scaloppina, on top of ham. Fold sides and end pieces of scaloppina over filling and roll up snugly, then secure with a toothpick.

3. Heat ⅓ cup oil in a large, heavy skillet. Working in batches, brown involtini on all sides over medium-high heat until very brown, about 5 minutes per batch. Transfer browned involtini to a heavy pan large enough to hold them in one layer. Season to taste with salt and pepper.

4. When all involtini are cooked, add onions to skillet and sauté over medium heat for about 2 minutes, stirring with a wooden spoon. (Add a bit more oil if necessary.) Add tomato paste and cook for 30 seconds more, then add rosemary and 3 cups of water. Bring to a boil, reduce heat to medium-low, and simmer for 5 minutes. Pour sauce over involtini in their pan, then lightly sprinkle flour over involtini and sauce. Cook, partially covered, over medium-low heat until veal is very tender, about 1½ hours. After first 15 minutes, stir involtini often to prevent them from sticking to bottom of pan. The flour will dissolve and thicken sauce.

5. Transfer involtini to a serving dish, remove toothpicks, and spoon sauce over them.

Mountain Splendor

Rightly or wrongly, no other herb is so immediately and indelibly associated with Italian cooking as is oregano (*Origanum vulgare*). According to one theory, the word itself derives from the Greek *oros* (mountain) and *ganos* (splendor), a reference to its native habitat and a tribute to its flavor or perhaps simply to its luminous gray-green color. In any case, the Greeks considered it a symbol of peace. The Italians, on the other hand, who call it *origano*, consider it an all but essential accent for tomato and eggplant dishes and also use it widely with fish. A wild perennial of the mint family, oregano grows especially well in central and southern Italy. Traditionally, it is harvested by hand, tied into bunches, and dried in the shade. Although some recipes do call for it fresh, Italians tend to prefer oregano in its dried form, finding it less bitter—and, of course, more readily available year-round.

Bistecca alla Pizzaiola

(Pizzaiolo's Wife's Steak)

SERVES 2

TRADITION SUGGESTS that this hearty dish—based on an oregano-flavored tomato sauce—was invented by the wives of the pizza makers, or *pizzaioli*, of Naples.

2 ¾"-thick T-bone or
   shell steaks
Salt and freshly ground
   black pepper
2 tbsp. extra-virgin
   olive oil
2 cloves garlic, peeled
¼ tsp. red pepper flakes
Leaves from 3 sprigs fresh
   or dried oregano,
   chopped or crumbled
½ cup white wine
1 cup tomato sauce
   (see page 90, steps
   1 and 2), puréed in a
   blender or food processor
3 sprigs fresh Italian
   parsley, chopped

1. Season steaks on both sides with salt and pepper. Heat oil in a large, heavy skillet over medium-high heat until hot but not smoking. Add garlic and sauté for 1 minute, then add steaks. Quickly brown steaks for 1 minute on each side, then transfer to a warmed plate. Add red pepper flakes and oregano to hot pan, then add wine and cook, stirring with a wooden spoon, until liquid is slightly reduced, about 1 minute. Add tomato sauce, stir, then return steaks to pan. Reduce heat to medium and cook for 6–8 minutes, turning steaks once, halfway through. Add a little water to sauce if it is too thick.

2. Put steaks on a serving dish, pour sauce over steaks, and garnish with parsley.

Tagliata di Manzo

(Sliced Grilled Steak)

SERVES 4

WHEN Marcella Hazan (left, outside a Venetian butcher shop) made lunch for us at her home in Venice, before she moved back to the U.S., this simple dish was the main course.

⅓ cup extra-virgin
   olive oil
12 cloves garlic, peeled
2 sprigs fresh rosemary
2 boneless rib-eye or strip
   steaks, 2" thick
Salt and freshly ground
   black pepper

1. Heat oil and garlic in a medium sauté pan over medium-high heat. Cook, stirring occasionally, until garlic is pale gold, about 7 minutes. Remove from heat and add rosemary sprigs, turning them over several times, then set pan (with garlic and rosemary) aside.

2. Heat a large cast-iron skillet or stove-top grill over high heat. When skillet is very hot, add steaks, which should sizzle instantly and quickly begin to smoke. Cook until very brown on one side, 2–3 minutes, then turn steaks over, sprinkle with salt, and cook for another 3 minutes (the steaks should be very rare).

3. Remove skillet from heat and transfer steaks to a cutting board. Slice them on an angle, across the grain, into ½"-thick slices.

4. Return pan with garlic and rosemary to stove and heat over medium-high heat. When oil begins to heat up, add steak slices, together with any juices on cutting board. Cook for about 1 minute, turning frequently and seasoning generously with black pepper. Adjust salt if necessary.

A Nice Chianina

With occasional exceptions—like tagliata di manzo (above) or the bistecca alla pizzaiola on the previous pages—steak dishes are not hugely popular with Italians. And although Italian veal is famous the world around, Italian beef, in general, boasts no particular reputation. There is one big exception, closely associated with one other Italian steak dish: chianina. That's the name of the celebrated former draft animal first bred for meat in Tuscany's Val di Chiana in the mid-19th century and now considered essential by connoisseurs for bistecca alla fiorentina—the heroic charcoal-grilled T-bone, typically an inch and a half thick and weighing nearly two pounds (including bone), that is one of the purest expressions of Tuscan gastronomy. (A steak this size, it should be noted, is meant to feed at least two diners, if not three.) A pedant might point out, however, that the chianina cattle likely to end up as bistecca alla fiorentina aren't exactly beef; technically, they're vitellone, large veal calves, slaughtered between the ages of one and two years, before they've had time to accumulate much fat. With *mucca pazza*, or mad cow disease, having now spread to Italian cattle, the government has prohibited the sale of T-bone steak—putting la fiorentina at risk of becoming a lost culinary tradition.

Venison Osso Buco

Lidia Bastianich (see page 162) gave us this variation on the classic osso buco. Cook 2 chopped, peeled medium yellow onions in ¼ cup of extra-virgin olive oil in a large pot over medium-high heat until soft, about 5 minutes. Add 1 shredded, peeled medium carrot, 1 rib chopped celery, 1 bay leaf, 4 cloves, 1 sprig fresh rosemary, and 10 juniper berries and season to taste with salt and freshly ground black pepper. Cook until vegetables are golden, about 15 minutes; transfer to a bowl and set aside. Generously salt six 8–10-oz. venison shanks (cut from hind shanks), then lightly dredge in flour. Add 2 tbsp. olive oil to same pot and sear shanks until browned on all sides, about 10 minutes. Return vegetables to pot, reduce heat to medium, add 2 tsp. tomato paste, and cook until tomato paste begins to caramelize, about 6 minutes. Add 1 cup fruity red wine (such as chianti) and bring to a boil, scraping up any brown bits stuck to bottom of pot. Add 1 cup fresh carrot juice, the zest of 1 lemon, and the zest and juice of 1 orange. Bring to a vigorous boil and cook until sauce has reduced and vegetables have softened, about 8 minutes. Add 6

peeled and crushed plum tomatoes, reduce heat to medium-low, and simmer, uncovered, for 30 minutes. Stir in 2 cups of hot chicken stock, partially cover pot, and simmer until meat is fork tender, about 1½ hours. Remove meat from pot, then strain sauce. Return meat to pot with sauce and keep warm until ready to serve.

Osso Buco
(Braised Veal Shank)

SERVES 4

ITALIAN RESTAURANTS in America sometimes offer pasta or risotto as a side dish. This practice is unknown in Italy—with one exception: the happy pairing of osso buco with risotto alla milanese in the restaurants of Lombardy.

½ cup extra-virgin
  olive oil
1 leek, white part only,
  washed, trimmed, and
  minced
3 medium carrots, peeled,
  trimmed, and minced
2 ribs celery, trimmed and
  minced
2 sprigs fresh rosemary
2 leaves fresh sage
1 2"-strip lemon zest
1 cup tomato sauce
  (see page 90, steps
  1 and 2)
1 cup brodo di carne (see
  page 76) or beef stock
2 3-lb. whole veal shanks,
  each cut into 4 pieces
Salt and freshly ground
  black pepper
1 cup flour

1. Preheat oven to 350°. Heat ¼ cup of the oil in a large, heavy pot with cover over medium heat. Add leeks, carrots, celery, rosemary, and sage and cook, stirring, until vegetables are golden brown, about 15 minutes. Stir in lemon peel, tomato sauce, and broth. Remove from heat and set aside.

2. Meanwhile, generously season veal shanks with salt and pepper, then dredge them in flour until lightly coated, shaking off excess flour. Heat remaining ¼ cup oil in a large skillet over medium-high heat. Add veal shanks and sear, turning once, until well browned on both sides, about 5 minutes per side. Place veal shanks in pot with vegetables, cover, and transfer to oven. Cook until meat is fork tender and falling off the bone, about 2 hours. Serve with risotto alla milanese (see recipe, page 145).

Coda alla Vaccinara

(Roman Stewed Oxtail)

SERVES 4

SABATINI on the piazza Santa Maria in Trastevere (left) serves a hearty version of this traditional Roman preparation—oxtail as cooked by the butcher's wife, or *vaccinara*.

¼ cup extra-virgin
  olive oil
2 oz. fat from prosciutto
  or fatty salt pork, finely
  chopped
1 small white onion,
  peeled and finely
  chopped
1 carrot, peeled, trimmed,
  and finely chopped
4 ribs celery, 1 rib finely
  chopped, 3 cut crosswise
  into thirds and blanched
2 lbs. meaty oxtail,
  cut into pieces 2½" to
  3" thick
1¼ cups chianti or other
  dry Italian red wine
1 28-oz. can whole peeled
  Italian plum tomatoes
Salt and freshly ground
  black pepper

1. Put oil, prosciutto fat, onions, carrots, and chopped celery rib into a large, heavy casserole and sauté over medium-high heat, stirring frequently, until fat has rendered and vegetables are soft, about 5 minutes.

2. Add oxtail and cook until lightly browned, stirring vegetables often, about 5 minutes. Add wine and cook, scraping browned bits stuck to bottom of casserole with a wooden spoon, until liquid has reduced by a quarter, 6–8 minutes.

3. Add tomatoes and their juices. Season to taste with salt and pepper, reduce heat to medium-low, cover, and simmer, stirring occasionally to break up tomatoes, for 2 hours. Add blanched celery pieces, cover again, and continue simmering until meat is very tender, about 1 hour more.

The Fifth Quarter

T he Testaccio market, on the south-eastern edge of old Rome," reports writer David Downie, who lived in Rome as a child, "gets its character from the fact that for hundreds of years it was the site of the city's most important slaughter-house. Even though the slaughterhouse has moved to the suburbs, Testaccio is still full of market stalls and food shops. It's also the hub around which establishments like Checchino dal 1887, Perilli, and Lo Scopet-taro are grouped—restaurants known for Rome's gutsy *quinto quarto* cooking. The words literally mean "fifth fourth" and refer to the organ meats and other nonstandard items—brains, sweetbreads, tripe, tails, even testicles—left over when the animal is dressed and quartered for sale. Ninetta Ceccacci Mariani, owner of century-old Checchino, explains that in the days before refrigeration, organ meats were difficult to keep fresh, and slaughterhouse workers received the quinto quarto as part of their pay. This gave rise to popular recipes based on such specialty items, many of which remain popular in Rome to this day, in Testaccio and elsewhere."

Roman Spring

Suckling lamb, *abbacchio* in Italian, has been the object of what might be called a Roman culinary cult for millennia, reports David Downie. Even Juvenal sang the praises of "the tenderest of the flock, with more milk than blood, that has not lost its virginity by eating grass". Ideally, says Downie, the abbacchio should be between 30 and 60 days old and have lost most of its baby fat without becoming tough. "According to Roman butcher Luciano Trabucchi," he continues, "there is no set weight for abbacchio; it depends on the breed and can range from about 12 pounds to 16 or 17." All breeds of lamb are good, he says—but for Easter, he greatly prefers abbacchio romanesco, raised on ancient pastureland near Rome. Abbacchio used to be strictly a springtime treat, but with an international supply now available, it can be had year-round. Nevertheless, maintains Aurelio Mariani, owner of Antico Ristorante Pagnanelli in Castel Gandolfo, "it's an Easter dish." The term *abbacchio* derives from the verb *abbacchiare*, "to beat down or demoralize"—in turn derived from *bacchio*, or "long stick". It is possible that suckling lambs were once clubbed to death with a similar implement. But a kinder etymology is possible: abbacchiare also means to sell at bargain-basement prices—to dump on the market. Baby lambs are abundant in spring, and that drives down prices. As Ninetta Ceccacci Mariani of Checchino dal 1887 explains, "Baby lambs used to come pouring onto the market all at once, because lamb was raised seasonally. The land can support only so many sheep, so eating the lambs around Eastertime made sense because they were available and affordable."

Abbacchio al Forno con Patate

(Roast Suckling Lamb with Potatoes)

SERVES 8

SINCE ABBACCHIO used to be something of a rarity, available only in springtime, Romans have traditionally eaten every bit of it—including, at least prior to recent food scares, the head, which is considered to be especially flavorful.

1 12–15-lb. whole lamb
  (have butcher cut lamb
  into quarters and crack
  all joints)
⅓ cup extra-virgin
  olive oil
3 heads garlic, separated
  into cloves and peeled
1½ cups fresh rosemary
  leaves
Salt and freshly ground
  black pepper
4 lbs. small potatoes
2 cups dry white wine

1. Preheat oven to 375°. Rinse lamb under running water. Pat lamb dry, then trim any excess fat, leaving a very thin layer to protect meat while cooking. Rub lamb lightly with 2 tbsp. of the oil.

2. Using a paring knife, make small incisions all over lamb. Cut about half of the garlic into thick slices and slip them into incisions along with about half of the rosemary leaves. Season lamb all over with salt.

3. Place lamb, bone side down, in a large roasting pan, leaving plenty of room for potatoes (to be added later). Slightly crush remaining garlic, scatter over lamb, and roast for 45 minutes.

4. Quarter potatoes, toss with remaining rosemary and oil, and scatter around lamb, stirring to coat with pan juices. Pour wine over lamb and continue roasting, basting with pan juices, until meat is cooked (it is traditionally served well done), about another 45 minutes.

5. Remove lamb from oven, transfer to a platter, and allow to rest for 20 minutes. Return potatoes to oven and cook until potatoes are tender, about 15 minutes. To serve, cut lamb at joints. Moisten meat with pan juices, adjust seasoning, and serve with potatoes.

Fegato alla Veneziana

(Venetian Calf's Liver and Onions)

SERVES 6

EVERYONE WE ASKED told us that Harry's Bar served the definitive fegato alla veneziana. We tried it there and at lots of other places, and we agree. This is Harry's recipe.

---

2 lbs. calf's liver,
   trimmed, thin membrane
   peeled off
6 tbsp. extra-virgin
   olive oil
6 small yellow onions,
   peeled, halved, and very
   thinly sliced
Salt and freshly ground
   black pepper
3 tbsp. butter
½ bunch Italian parsley,
   trimmed and chopped

1. Cut liver lengthwise into 4 long pieces, then, using a very sharp knife and pressing the palm of your hand firmly against the meat, slice each piece crosswise into pieces as thin as possible.

2. Heat 4 tbsp. of the oil in a large skillet over medium heat. Add onions and cook, stirring frequently, until soft and deep golden brown, about 20 minutes. Transfer onions with a slotted spoon to a bowl and set aside.

3. Increase heat to medium-high and add remaining 2 tbsp. oil. When oil is sizzling hot, add liver in batches, so as not to overcrowd the skillet, and cook, stirring constantly with a wooden spoon, until brown and crispy on edges, 3–5 minutes. Season liberally with salt and pepper, then add reserved onions and accumulated juices. Cook for 2 minutes, stirring and turning liver and onions constantly while shaking skillet over heat. Transfer to a heated serving platter.

4. Add butter to skillet and scrape up any brown bits stuck to bottom of skillet as butter melts. Remove skillet from heat and stir in parsley. Spoon butter and parsley over liver and onions. Serve with grilled polenta (see page 150), if you like.

Harry the American

Serious restaurant critics sometimes criticize Harry's Bar and its offspring, complaining that the food is too ordinary and the surroundings too casual to merit such high prices. But, says SAVEUR editor Colman Andrews, "however heart stopping the tariff, never once have I walked away feeling that I haven't gotten more than my money's worth." Harry's dates from 1931. One Giuseppe Cipriani, a bartender at the Hotel Europa in Venice, had lent money to a dipsomaniacal young American habitué named Harry Pickering. Pickering used the loan to go back to the States—and then surprised everybody by returning to pay back Cipriani's loan with interest. The sum was enough to bankroll a bar, which the two named Harry's. Over the years, while remaining one of the world's great watering holes, Harry's developed into a first-rate restaurant, too, now under the direction of Giuseppe's son Arrigo (facing page, top)— Arrigo being more or less the Italian version of Harry, allowing him to claim that he's the only man who has ever been named after a bar.

Trippa alle Verdure

(Stewed Tripe with Vegetables)

SERVES 8

NATALE RUSCONI notes that peas or green beans may be added to this dish, and that it may be made ahead of time and frozen; just add some raw vegetables when reheating.

2 cups white vinegar
Salt
2–3 lbs. veal tripe
3 medium russet potatoes, peeled
2 carrots, peeled and trimmed
1 rib celery, trimmed and peeled
3 zucchini, trimmed
1 bunch Italian parsley, leaves finely chopped
Zest of 1 lemon
4 cloves garlic, peeled and minced
¼ cup extra-virgin olive oil
3 medium yellow onions, peeled and finely chopped
1 ripe medium tomato, cored, peeled, and chopped
1 red bell pepper, roasted, peeled, cored, and chopped
Freshly ground black pepper
2 cups white wine
4 cups brodo di carne (see page 76), or beef stock
6 tbsp. butter
1 cup freshly grated parmigiano-reggiano

1. Bring a large pot of water to a boil over high heat. Add vinegar and several generous pinches of salt, then plunge tripe in and allow water to return to a boil. Drain and rinse under cold water. Slice tripe into 4" × ½" pieces with a sharp knife, cover, and set aside.

2. Quarter potatoes lengthwise, then trim each piece with a paring knife into an ovoid shape, reserving trimmings. Put ovoid pieces into a bowl of cold water, then finely chop trimmings and set aside. Cut carrots, celery, and zucchini into 2" lengths and add to potatoes, again reserving trimmings. Finely chop vegetable trimmings and set aside. Combine parsley, lemon zest, and half of the garlic in a small bowl, then cover with plastic wrap and set aside.

3. Heat oil in a large, heavy pot over medium heat. Add onions and remaining garlic and cook until golden, 10–15 minutes. Add potato and vegetable trimmings, tomatoes, and peppers and season with salt and pepper to taste. Cook, stirring often, until soft, 5–10 minutes.

4. Add tripe and wine and cook until alcohol has evaporated, about 3 minutes. Add stock and two-thirds of all the vegetables and bring to a boil. Reduce heat to low, cover, and simmer until tripe is very tender, 4–6 hours. Add remaining potatoes, carrots, and celery about 1 hour before tripe is done. Add zucchini about 30 minutes later. Add parsley mixture, butter, and half the parmigiano. Adjust seasonings. Serve with remaining parmigiano.

The Hotelier at Home

Natale Rusconi (above), the urbane director of the Hotel Cipriani in Venice—the luxurious hostelry opened in 1958 on the Giudecca by Giuseppe Cipriani with the backing of Lord Iveagh of Guinness and now owned by James Sherwood's Orient-Express group—is no stranger to the kitchen. He began his hotel career apprenticing at the stoves at London's Savoy Hotel in 1954, and he still loves to cook. Whereas other hoteliers might treat honored guests to a special dinner in the hotel dining room, in fact, Rusconi likes to invite them to his little villa across the canal from the Cipriani and offer them a home-cooked meal. We enjoyed his generosity ourselves a few years back and helped trim vegetables as he prepared this excellent tripe dish—not particularly Venetian but very good.

Origins Unknown

Sitting and sharing culinary lore with me on the terrace of a seaside caffè," recalls SAVEUR editor Colman Andrews, "Linda Belforte, retired chef of Genoa's Yacht Club Italiano, suddenly and quite unintentionally reminded me of an old French specialty. She was describing one particularly complicated Genoese preparation involving various veal parts strung onto skewers with artichokes and other vegetables, coated in besciamella (béchamel) sauce, and...at that point I interrupted and said, 'And then you dip the skewers in an egg wash, dredge them in bread crumbs, and fry them?' 'Yes, exactly,' Belforte replied, not a little surprised. What she was describing, I realized, was almost exactly a genre of classical French preparations known as *attereaux*, or skewers. Were stecchi (the word means the same thing) a French invention adopted by the Genoese? Or did they originate in Genoa and travel to France, where they were elaborated upon? Because their ingredients are so typically Genoese, I'd suspect the latter. But when Belforte finally made them for me, they were so good, I didn't much care where they came from."

Stecchi
(Genoese Skewers)

SERVES 4

THIS COMPLEX Genoese specialty, French in form if not necessarily in origin, is typical of the special dishes Genoa's cooks prepared to welcome home returning sailors.

2 tbsp. extra-virgin
    olive oil
¼ lb. sweetbreads,
    membranes removed
Half a calf's brain
    (about ¼ lb.)
½ lb. loin of veal, cut into
    8 equal pieces
Salt and freshly ground
    black pepper
8 baby artichokes
1 small lemon, cut in half
2 small carrots, peeled and
    cut into 8 equal pieces
2 small zucchini, cut into
    8 equal pieces
8 tbsp. butter
2 cups flour
4 cups milk, warmed
Pinch freshly ground nutmeg
4 eggs, lightly beaten
1½ cups fine dried
    bread crumbs
8 small white mushrooms
Vegetable oil

1. Heat olive oil in a large skillet over medium-high heat. Sauté sweetbreads and brains together until just browned, 15–20 seconds per side. Transfer sweetbreads and brains to a plate and set aside. Add veal to skillet and sauté, stirring, until brown on all sides, about 4 minutes. Transfer veal to plate with brains and sweetbreads. Season meats with salt and pepper to taste.

2. Trim artichokes, removing tough outer leaves and cutting off stem and thorny top. Rub cut surfaces with lemon to keep from discoloring. Bring a small pot of salted water to a boil over high heat. Add carrots and cook for 5 minutes; add zucchini and continue cooking until tender, about 3 minutes. Remove vegetables with a slotted spoon and plunge into cold water. Add artichokes to boiling water and cook until tender, about 5 minutes. Drain and set aside.

3. Melt butter in a medium saucepan over low heat. Whisk in 1 cup flour and cook until thick and beginning to bubble, 1–2 minutes. Slowly whisk in milk. Increase heat to medium and cook, whisking, until sauce reaches a simmer, 7–10 minutes. Season with nutmeg and salt and pepper to taste and transfer to a shallow bowl. Place a piece of plastic wrap on surface of sauce to prevent "skin" from forming. Let cool to room temperature. Meanwhile, place eggs, bread crumbs, and remaining 1 cup of flour in 3 separate wide, shallow bowls.

4. To assemble stecchi, cut brains and sweetbreads into 8 pieces each; thread them, along with veal, carrots, zucchini, artichokes, and mushrooms onto 8" skewers, beginning with artichokes and finishing with mushrooms.

5. Coat skewers with sauce (it will be thick, so smooth it on with a spoon). Roll skewers in flour, then egg, then bread crumbs. Pour oil into a large, deep skillet to a depth of about 1" and heat over medium-high heat until hot but not smoking. Fry stecchi in batches until golden on all sides, 7–10 minutes. Drain on paper towels and sprinkle with salt.

VEGETABLES AND SIDE DISHES

"JUST PAST the garden at my house in

Tuscany, the grass yields to uncultivated

farmland, a tangle of broom, blackberry

vines, wildflowers—and wild fennel. As I

watch my children walk through this landscape in late summer, arms laden with the stalks and fronds of that most Florentine of vegetables, I am glad that for everything there is a season and that for this season there is fennel." —LORI ZIMRING DE MORI

Carciofi alla Giudia

(Jewish-Style Fried Whole Artichokes)

SERVES 6

THIS METHOD of cooking artichokes—in which the outer leaves turn wonderfully crisp while the heart, stem, and inner leaves remain tender—is the best-known example of Roman Jewish cuisine in the Eternal City today. Our recipe comes from a neighborhood eatery, Osteria ar Galletto.

6 long-stemmed artichokes
Half a lemon
Vegetable oil
Salt

1. To clean artichokes, pull off the tough green outer leaves until you get to the tender, pale yellowish leaves. Use a vegetable peeler to peel stems, then trim stems to about 1". Slice about 1" off tops of artichokes and use scissors to snip off the thorny tips of the leaves. Spread leaves open and use a spoon to scoop out fibrous white chokes. Rub all exposed surfaces of artichokes with lemon to prevent discoloration.

2. Pour vegetable oil into a heavy skillet to a depth of 3". Heat oil over medium-high heat. When oil is very hot but not smoking, about 375° on a candy thermometer, add 2 artichokes. Cook, turning until lightly browned, about 8 minutes. Drain on paper towels and repeat process with remaining artichokes.

3. Place each fried artichoke, stem side up, on a clean surface and flatten by pressing with a dinner plate. Return each artichoke to hot oil and cook again, turning until evenly golden brown and crisp, about 6 minutes. Drain on paper towels. Sprinkle with salt and serve whole.

A Cuisine Apart

Jewish traders are said to have arrived in Rome well before the birth of Christ, establishing a small community in the city. In the 16th century, Pope Paul IV walled in a portion of land between the Tiber and the Campidoglio, creating a Jewish ghetto, which eventually grew to a population of about 4,000. Largely isolated from their brethren elsewhere in Europe, the Roman Jews developed a cuisine that was neither Sephardic nor Ashkenazic but that drew on both, adding vivid Italian flavors. Besides fried artichokes, a typical Roman Jewish menu might include air-dried beef (in place of pork-based prosciutto), marinated fried fish, stracciatella (see page 71), and matzo-flour lasagne with lamb sauce.

Roman Pride

Shopping one day on the Campo de' Fiori, site of Rome's most picturesque marketplace, writer David Downie got into a conversation with a produce merchant known as "La Cicoriara", the Chicory Lady. La Cicoriara proudly told Downie that almost every vegetable has its "romanesco" version—the result of centuries of expert local farming. "And they're the best of their kind," she insisted, especially the round, blunt-leaved Roman artichokes. Brandishing a plump carciofo romanesco cimarolo, she explained that it is so named because it comes from the *cima*, or top, of the bush and is thus "the plant's firstborn". Cimaroli are sold by the piece, not the bunch, and cost much more than mere braccioli, artichokes grown on lower branches—which, says La Cicoriara, are "never quite as good".

Carciofi alla Romana
(Roman-Style Artichokes)

SERVES 6

IN ROME, these artichokes are seasoned with mentuccia, a delicate wild mint native to Italy. Purists argue that there's no substitute—but fresh, American-grown mint works fine.

6 long-stemmed artichokes
1 lemon, halved
¾ cup chopped fresh mint
   leaves
4 cloves garlic, peeled and
   minced
Salt
1 cup extra-virgin
   olive oil
2 cups frascati or other dry
   Italian white wine
Freshly ground black
   pepper

1. To clean artichokes, pull off the tough green outer leaves until you get to the tender, pale yellowish leaves. Use a vegetable peeler to peel stems, then trim stems to about 1". Slice about 1" off tops of artichokes and use scissors to snip off the thorny tips of the leaves. Spread leaves open and use a spoon to scoop out fibrous white chokes. Rub all exposed surfaces of artichokes with lemon to prevent discoloration.

2. Stir together mint, garlic, and 2 tsp. salt in a small bowl. Pack approximately 2 tbsp. mint mixture between leaves and rub a little in the center of each artichoke.

3. Pour ½ cup of the oil into a large deep pan. Place artichokes stem side up in saucepan and pour wine and remaining oil on top. Cover and cook over medium-low heat until tender (check for tenderness at thickest part of the stem), about 40 minutes. Season to taste with salt and pepper.

4. Transfer artichokes to a platter and allow to cool completely. (They are best when served at room temperature.) Continue to cook juices until reduced by half, then serve as a sauce, drizzled over artichokes. Store artichokes with reduced juices in refrigerator for up to 1 week.

Mercato di Sant'-Ambrogio

While Florence's famous Mercato di San Lorenzo is often overrun by tourists, the medium-size Mercato di Sant'Ambrogio (right) in the piazza Ghiberti is purely for the Florentines. From 7 A.M. farmers sell just-picked produce—piled up perfectly—to regular customers who crowd the market to pick out ingredients for the day's meals. Nestled in the middle of the market is one of Florence's best-kept secrets: a tiny *tavola calda*—a favorite lunch spot of local art students—serving a limited menu of home-style Tuscan dishes, made with ingredients hand-selected daily from market vendors.

Finocchio al Burro e Parmigiano

(Fennel with Butter and Parmigiano-Reggiano)

FENNEL IS ONE of the world's oldest known edible plants. A classic Italian method for preparing this aromatic vegetable is to cook it in butter and serve it with parmigiano.

Salt
8 *small bulbs of fennel,*
    trimmed and quartered
5 *tbsp. butter*
Freshly ground black
    pepper
¼ *cup freshly grated*
    parmigiano-reggiano

1. Bring a large pot of salted water to a boil over high heat. Add fennel and cook until slightly softened, about 5 minutes, then drain.

2. Heat butter in a large skillet over medium heat. Add fennel, season to taste with salt and pepper, and cook, turning fennel occasionally, until just tender, about 15 minutes. Transfer to a warm serving dish and sprinkle with parmigiano.

Finocchio Fritto

(Fried Fennel)

SERVES 6–8

THE BATTER in this recipe is adapted from one given in the encyclopedic 1891-vintage *La Scienza in Cucina e L'Arte di Mangiar Bene* (The Science of Cookery and the Art of Eating Well) by Pellegrino Artusi—one of the great Italian cookbooks. More recently, it was translated in the U.S. as *The Art of Eating Well* (Random House, 1996). This batter recipe may also be used for frying such vegetables as eggplant, mushrooms, squash blossoms, and zucchini.

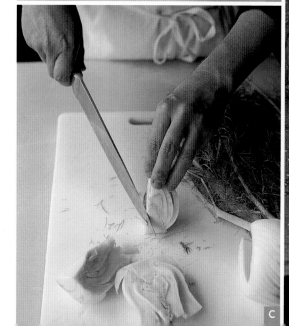

1 ¾ cups flour
Salt
1 egg, separated
1 tbsp. extra-virgin
 olive oil
2 tbsp. white wine
4 medium fennel bulbs,
 trimmed and cut into
 wedges
2 cups corn oil

1. Mix together ¾ cup of the flour and a generous pinch of salt in a medium bowl, then make a well in the center of the flour. Lightly beat egg yolk, olive oil, and wine in a small bowl, then pour into well. Stirring with a wooden spoon, gradually incorporate flour into liquid, then slowly add cold water (about 12 tbsp. in all), stirring constantly, until batter is smooth but still thick. Cover and refrigerate for at least 2 hours but no more than 12.

2. Bring a medium pot of salted water to a boil over high heat. Add fennel and cook until tender, 5–10 minutes. Use a slotted spoon to transfer fennel to paper towels to drain. Set fennel aside to let cool.

3. Whisk egg white in a medium mixing bowl until stiff (but not dry) peaks form, then fold into chilled batter with a rubber spatula. Heat corn oil in a large skillet over medium-high heat until hot but not smoking, about 375° on a candy thermometer. Put remaining 1 cup flour in a medium bowl, dredge fennel wedges, and shake off excess flour. Dip fennel in batter to coat completely, then carefully put into hot oil and fry, turning once or twice, until crispy and golden, 1–2 minutes per side. Use a slotted spoon to transfer fennel to paper towels to drain. Sprinkle liberally with salt and serve hot.

Using Fennel

As summer's bounty fades, fennel appears. No other vegetable is so versatile—and equally delicious—both raw (when it's crisp and assertively aromatic) and cooked (when its crunch mellows to a tender softness and its bold flavor becomes more delicate). In America, fennel is usually sold (often incorrectly labeled "anise") in its pared-down state: the bare bulb, with few stalks or fronds. But you may come across the whole vegetable (A), perhaps at a farmers' market, and it's easy to prepare; leaving the core intact is the key to easy cutting. Begin by trimming a ¼" piece from the root end, then slice off the stalks about 1" above the bulb (B). Reserve the fronds and pull away any blemished outer pieces. For fennel wedges, quarter the trimmed bulb and cut out the centermost piece of core, leaving the wedge intact (C). Experiment with other cuts: chop the fronds and use them to flavor dishes; a trimmed, whole bulb may be sliced lengthwise into flat pieces; the quartered fennel may be sliced into smaller wedges or cut crosswise into strips.

Cicoria in Padella

(Pan-Fried Chicory)

SERVES 4

WE LEARNED this typical Roman method of cooking greens from Sabatini, on the piazza Santa Maria in Trastevere, one of the prettiest old squares in the Eternal City.

2 lbs. escarole, curly
    endive, or other chicory,
    well washed and
    trimmed
3 tbsp. extra-virgin
    olive oil
1 clove garlic, crushed
    and peeled
1–2 pinches red pepper
    flakes
Salt

1. Bring a large pot of salted water to a boil over high heat. Add escarole and cook until well wilted, about 5 minutes. Drain well, rinse in cold water, and drain well again.

2. Heat oil, garlic, and red pepper flakes in a large skillet over medium-high heat until fragrant, about 1 minute. Add greens, season to taste with salt, and sauté until liquid evaporates, about 5 minutes.

Italian Fire

Peperoncini, or red pepper flakes, aren't just some latter-day pizza-parlor cliché. They have been used in Italian cooking since the arrival of the capsicums from the New World in the 16th century. Peperoncini have always been particularly popular in southern Italy: Calabria, traditionally one of the poorest regions in the country, is especially generous in its use of red pepper flakes, perhaps because they helped perk up the monotonous diet of earlier times. Even in Rome, though, in more or less the middle of Italy, peperoncini are a common accent: for instance, in pasta cooked all'arrabbiata ("angry style") or alla puttanesca ("whore's style") and in simple sautéed greens.

Delicious Circle

Genoa's most famous thoroughfare, the broad and stately via Garibaldi, may well have been the first totally planned European street. Begun in 1551, it was built with all its perspectives worked out in advance, and all the Renaissance-style palaces that line it were designed to ideal proportions. One of these, the Palazzo Spinola, is home today to the oldest men's club in the city, the Circolo Artistico Tunnel—the Tunnel Artistic Club (hilly Genoa is honeycombed with tunnels)—founded in 1891. Everything in the dining room at the club (above), under the direction of Gianni Belforte, is done with high style and attention to detail. The food—from classic trenette al pesto to baroque cappon magro (see page 48) to simply cooked fish and meat—is superb, with impeccably trained waiters in white gloves serving members at tables draped with creamy linens and set with gleaming silver. Just before service begins, though, the staff sits in a far simpler setting for a homier meal, perhaps including a polpettone. Everyone eats well in Italy.

Polpettone di Patate e Fagiolini

(Crustless Potato and Green Bean Tart)

SERVES 6–8

IN ITALIAN, *polpetta* means croquette; a *polpettone* is a big croquette—but in this case it is baked, not fried. This dish, which can be made from any number or combination of vegetables, is a classic example of Genoese home cooking.

1 lb. boiling potatoes, peeled and sliced
Salt
¾ lb. green beans, trimmed
1 cup fine fresh bread crumbs
¾ cup milk
¼ cup extra-virgin olive oil
2 cloves garlic, peeled and minced
2 tbsp. finely chopped fresh oregano
2 tbsp. finely chopped fresh Italian parsley
¾ cup freshly grated parmigiano-reggiano
¼ cup ricotta
4 eggs, lightly beaten
Freshly ground black pepper

1. Preheat oven to 350°. Place potatoes in a medium saucepan of cold salted water and simmer over medium-high heat until tender, about 20 minutes. Drain, mash with a fork (a few lumps are okay), and cover to keep warm.

2. Meanwhile, bring another medium saucepan of salted water to a boil over high heat. Add green beans and cook until tender, about 15 minutes. Drain, finely chop, and set aside.

3. Soak bread crumbs in milk in a small bowl. Heat 2 tbsp. of the oil in a small skillet over medium heat. Add garlic and cook until fragrant, about 2 minutes. Add oregano, parsley, and green beans and continue cooking for about 2 minutes longer. Transfer mixture to a large bowl and stir in potatoes. Add parmigiano, ricotta, and eggs. Season with salt and pepper and mix thoroughly.

4. Spoon potato mixture into an 8" x 11" rectangular or 12" round baking pan and smooth with a spatula. Top with bread crumbs, score top, and bake until golden, about 40 minutes. Serve warm or at room temperature. Drizzle with remaining oil.

Radicchio Tardivo di Treviso al Forno

(Baked Late-Season Radicchio di Treviso)

SERVES 6

THE BEAUTIFUL lean-ribbed late-season radicchio from the region of Treviso, in the Veneto countryside, is sometimes available in America. If you can't find it, Marcella Hazan recommends substituting Belgian endive, which has a similar crisp bitterness, instead of leafy round radicchio.

5 *thick heads radicchio*
  tardivo di treviso or
  6 heads Belgian endive
Salt and freshly ground
  black pepper
6 tbsp. extra-virgin
  olive oil

1. Preheat oven to 400°. Discard any bruised or wilted outer leaves from radicchio heads and cut off discolored root ends. Wash under cold running water and shake off moisture. (If using Belgian endive, trim away a thin slice from the stem end to ensure even cooking and discard any bruised or wilted outer leaves.)

2. Cut each head of radicchio or endive in half lengthwise, then make a V cut in the root end, cutting half as deep as the root is thick and running the cut from the bottom to the point where the leaves join the root.

3. Arrange radicchio or endive halves cut side up in a baking pan, overlapping if necessary. Season generously with salt and pepper and drizzle with 4 tbsp. of the oil. Bake for about 12 minutes, then turn radicchio over. Bake for another 8 minutes, then turn radicchio again so that the cut side is facing up. Drizzle with remaining 2 tbsp. oil and bake until the root end is tender when pierced with a knife, about 2 minutes more. Serve hot or warm.

Big Red

 singularly flavorful member of the chicory family, radicchio (*Cichorium intybus*) is a vibrantly colorful creature, with a smooth texture and a refined flavor, delicate with a hint of bitterness. Italians use it widely not just in salad bowls but also grilled or sautéed as a vegetable course or antipasto or mixed into pasta sauces and risottos. Radicchio was developed from a number of local chicory varieties in the Veneto region in the late 1860s by visiting Belgian garden consultant Francesco Van Den Borre. Today about a dozen different types of radicchio are grown in Italy, the two most common being the familiar rosa di chioggia, with its tight, red-and-white, cabbage-shaped head—a salad green that has become ubiquitous in America, even at McDonald's—and the elongated radicchio di treviso, which many connoisseurs prefer for its sweeter flavor.

Clove Story

Garlic (*Allium sativum*) is an essential ingredient in the cooking of Italy. But while it flavors the cuisine, it rarely takes center stage. With only a handful of exceptions, it is an accent, an elusive perfume—not the overbearing, searing aggressor it too often becomes in Italian-American food. When it comes to buying, using, and preserving garlic, here are some things that every Italian cook knows:

◆ **BUYING GARLIC:** Look for a firm bulb with tight skin. Do not use garlic that is mushy or blemished. If there are green shoots growing from the cloves, the garlic is old—but it is still usable; just split the cloves lengthwise and pull out the bitter green.

◆ **PEELING GARLIC:** Separate the cloves, then lay them flat, one at a time, on a cutting board. Crush cloves with steady but gentle pressure with the flat side of a knife blade. The papery peel will then easily pull away from the clove.

◆ **GETTING A MORE DELICATE FLAVOR:** Add the garlic to oil or sauces unpeeled, or just lightly crush the skins.

◆ **STORING GARLIC:** Best kept in a cool, dry place, away from direct light. Keep peeled garlic in a glass container in the refrigerator.

Funghi Trifolati
(Sautéed Mushrooms)

SERVES 6

IN PIEDMONTESE dialect, *trifola* means truffle; this and certain other dishes cooked with garlic (kidneys, for example) were originally called "truffled" because garlic's scent was thought to resemble that of the precious tuber.

1 ½ lbs. wild or cultivated
  mushrooms, trimmed
½ cup extra-virgin
  olive oil
2 cloves garlic, peeled and
  minced
Salt and freshly ground
  black pepper
½ cup chopped fresh
  Italian parsley

1. Carefully separate mushroom stems from caps and set caps aside. Trim off and discard ends of stems, then slice stems in half lengthwise. Wipe caps with a damp paper towel to remove any dirt.

2. Heat oil in a large, heavy skillet over medium-high heat. Add the garlic and cook, stirring constantly, until softened but not browned, about 1 minute, then remove and discard garlic.

3. Add mushroom caps and stems, increase heat to high, and cook, turning mushrooms often until the oil has been absorbed and the mushrooms have yielded and then reabsorbed all their juices, about 10 minutes. Season to taste with salt and pepper. Add parsley, shaking the pan to mix parsley and mushrooms together. Serve hot or at room temperature.

Cime di Rapa Affogate alla Pugliese

(Pugliese-Style Broccoli Rabe with Wine Sauce)

SERVES 4–6

AFFOGATE literally means "drowned", a reference to the process of cooking broccoli rabe in wine. This dish may also be made with broccolini, spinach, chicory, or any other greens.

½ cup extra-virgin
  olive oil
2 bunches broccoli rabe,
  ends trimmed
Salt
1 clove garlic, peeled
2 bay leaves
⅓ cup dry white wine
Freshly ground black
  pepper

1. Heat 2 tbsp. of the oil in a large sauté pan over medium heat. Rinse broccoli rabe under cold water and add to pan. Season to taste with salt, cover, and cook for 10 minutes, stirring occasionally so broccoli rabe does not stick.

2. Drain most of the accumulated liquid out of the pan, and add garlic, bay leaves, wine, and remaining 6 tbsp. of oil. Season to taste with salt and pepper. Reduce heat to medium-low and continue to cook until the liquid has been absorbed and broccoli rabe is tender, about 20 minutes more.

VARIATION—Bring a large pot of salted water to a boil over high heat. Add 2 bunches, trimmed broccoli rabe and cook until stalks are soft, about 5 minutes. Drain and set aside. Heat 6 tbsp. extra-virgin olive oil, 6 crushed and peeled garlic cloves, and a pinch of red pepper flakes in a large skillet over medium heat until garlic is golden, 3–4 minutes. Add drained broccoli rabe, season to taste with salt, and cook, stirring often, until liquid has evaporated and broccoli rabe is very soft, about 5 minutes.

The Bitter and the Sweet

When October arrives, Italian markets fill with staple winter vegetables, among them broccoletti and cime di rapa, or broccoli rabe—which are not at all the same thing. Both have skinny stems and flowering heads, but broccoletti is a type of broccoli with small, sweet buds (which explains why it's called "little broccoli" and why it tastes a lot like its namesake), while cime di rapa, literally "turnip tops", (also called rapini in Tuscany or broccoli di rape in Campania) is the flower shoot of a turnip and has a pungent, bitter taste. Neither vegetable, incidentally, is the same as broccolini, which is a hybrid of two kinds of broccoli.

Melanzane alla Parmigiana

(Eggplant Parmesan)

ONE OF ITALY'S most famous vegetable dishes, eggplant parmesan is best made with regular globe eggplants, not their larger cousins or the elongated Asian varieties.

2 medium-large eggplants
2 tbsp. salt
1 cup extra-virgin olive oil
Freshly ground black pepper
2 cups tomato sauce (see page 90, steps 1 and 2)
½ lb. fresh mozzarella, thinly sliced
6–8 fresh basil leaves
½ cup grated parmigiano-reggiano

1. Preheat oven to 375°. Slice eggplants lengthwise, about ½" thick, and salt generously on both sides. Place slices in a colander and set aside to drain for 1 hour. Brush salt off eggplant and pat each slice dry with a paper towel.

2. Heat oil in a large skillet over medium-high heat and fry eggplant in batches, turning once, until soft and golden, 4–5 minutes per side. As each batch is done, remove from skillet with tongs and drain on a wire rack. Season to taste with salt and pepper.

3. Spread a large spoonful of red sauce over the bottom of a shallow 8" x 10" baking dish and cover with a layer of eggplant slices. Tear about a third of the mozzarella slices into small pieces and scatter over the eggplant, then spread another large spoonful of red sauce over eggplant and mozzarella. Repeat layers with remaining eggplant slices, mozzarella, and red sauce, ending with a layer of red sauce.

4. Top assembled eggplant with basil leaves, then sprinkle parmigiano over the top and bake until cheese is bubbling around the edges and sauce has slightly caramelized on top, 20–25 minutes.

A Defining Matter

Technically speaking, many recipes "alla parmigiana" would be more accurately called "al parmigiano". Theoretically, "alla parmigiana" should mean "cooked Parma style"; however, this term is applied to many dishes that have no relation whatsoever to the traditional cuisine of Parma. Instead, "alla parmigiana" refers to perhaps the most influential product of Parma—and the essential ingredient of this dish—parmigiano-reggiano. This may explain why melanzane alla parmigiana is sometimes also called parmigiana di melanzane.

BREADS, TORTE, AND PIZZA

"'THERE ARE no secrets,' Don Antonio

Condurro assures me, brushing flour from

his smock near the old brick oven at Da

Michele (near right), his pizzeria in the Tribunali quarter of Naples—pizza's native city. 'Anyone who says there are secrets to making pizza is trying to be mysterious. It's just experience.'"—DAVID DOWNIE

Pizza Dough

MAKES 2 12" PIZZAS

NEAPOLITAN pizzaiolo Alfonso Carusone (right), who made surprisingly authentic Naples-style pizza at Tony May's late, lamented Hostaria in New York's Westchester County, let us watch him work and helped us develop this recipe.

1 7-gram packet active
   dry yeast
1 ½ cups all-purpose flour
1 ½ cups cake flour
1 tsp. salt
Extra-virgin olive oil
½ cup cornmeal

1. Dissolve yeast in ¼ cup lukewarm water in a large bowl. Set aside until yeast begins to activate (it will foam a little), about 10 minutes. Combine all-purpose and cake flours and salt in a small bowl. Add 1 cup flour mixture to yeast and stir well with a wooden spoon or your hands. Mix in ½ cup water, then add another cup flour and continue to stir. Add remaining 1 cup flour, then gradually stir in about ¼ cup water and mix well. The dough should be fairly soft but not too wet.

2. Turn out dough on a lightly floured surface and knead with the heels of your palms until it has a smooth, uniform texture, about 10–12 minutes. Divide dough into 2 even or equal balls. Coat the insides of 2 medium bowls with ½ tsp. oil each. Place dough in bowls, cover bowls with damp cloths or plastic wrap, and set aside to let rise until doubled in bulk, about 2½–3 hours.

3. Place pizza stone or unglazed tiles in oven and preheat at highest setting (not broil). Sprinkle a baker's peel or inverted baking sheet with cornmeal. Punch down dough from one bowl, make a ball, and flatten it on the peel or sheet. (Make sure the dough does not adhere to peel; otherwise it will not slide off easily.) Taking care not to overwork dough, stretch it into a thin 12" circle with a slightly raised edge. Add margherita or marinara topping (see recipe, page 266) and slide onto hot pizza stone.

4. Bake until crust is golden brown and crisp, about 12–15 minutes. Meanwhile, prepare second pizza. Remove first pizza from oven and bake the second on the same stone. Drizzle a little olive oil on each and serve.

Pizza Gospel

There are those who say that the celebrated baker Publius Paquius Proculus of ancient Pompeii made pizza before Vesuvius blew its top in A.D. 79", says writer David Downie. "If he did, he sure didn't use tomato sauce (tomatoes weren't eaten much in Naples until the 19th century)—and anyway, the word *pizza* didn't appear in print until 900 years later. Today, in any case, countless pizza ovens in the densely populated Naples *centro storico* pour plumes of smoke into the air, scenting the city with the aromas of burning oak and baking dough. You breathe pizza—almost literally—in Naples. You eat it as soon as you're weaned. You fold it over hot from curbside stalls and wolf it down on the way to school. You nibble it on your first date. Pizza lives in Neapolitan poetry, song, and literature—and in the city's largely untranslatable street jive. *Farsi una pizza*, one popular expression, suggests that this age-old food is a drug, to be 'done'. *Una vera pizza*, 'the real thing', means the best in Naples—which is to say the best in the world."

Fit for a Queen

A t his fabled Naples pizzeria, Brandi—which has been in the family since 1780—affable pizza kingpin Don Vincenzo Pagnani tells the story of how this quintessential Neapolitan pizza came to be. One day, he says, the humble pizzaiolo Raffaele Esposito—Pagnani's great-grandfather—was called to cater a royal feast for Queen Margherita di Savoia. To the classic marinara sauce he boldly added mozzarella cheese and basil leaves, to create an homage to the red, white, and green of Italy's flag. Asked by the monarch for the name of his new creation, Esposito diplomatically responded, "Margherita, Your Majesty!"

Margherita Topping

For 2 12" Pizzas

A NEAPOLITAN classic, pizza margherita has an official birth date: June 11, 1889. Ripe tomatoes are best for the sauce; if your tomatoes lack flavor, add tomato purée.

2 lbs. very ripe fresh
  plum tomatoes
Salt
16 small fresh basil leaves
  (or larger ones torn
  into pieces)
¼ cup extra-virgin
  olive oil
½ cup tomato purée
  (optional)
½ lb. fresh mozzarella,
  sliced

1. Core and stem tomatoes and make a small cross incision on the bottom of each, then plunge them into a large pot of boiling water for about 1 minute to loosen skins. Remove tomatoes from pot with a slotted spoon and transfer them to a large bowl of ice water. Peel tomatoes, discarding skins, and cut them in half crosswise. Squeeze out and discard seeds, then chop finely.

2. Place tomatoes in a colander, sprinkle with salt, and drain for 20 minutes. Transfer to a medium bowl, stir in basil and oil (and tomato purée, if using), and adjust seasoning. Spread tomato mixture evenly over pizza dough (see master pizza dough recipe, page 265), place mozzarella slices on top, and bake at highest setting for 12–15 minutes.

VARIATION—For marinara topping, omit the basil and mozzarella and substitute 4 small cloves garlic, peeled and minced, and leaves from 2 sprigs fresh oregano.

Calzone

(Cheese-and-Tomato-Filled Turnovers)

MAKES 4

THIS INSIDE-OUT pizza, whose name means "trouser leg" (for its shape), is a specialty of Naples. Calzone begs to be eaten with your hands—the way pizza was originally.

1 7-gram packet active dry yeast
1 ½ cups all-purpose flour
1 ½ cups cake flour
1 tsp. salt
Extra-virgin olive oil
½ cup cornmeal
½ lb. fresh mozzarella, sliced into 8 pieces
16 oil-packed anchovy filets
1 14-oz. can peeled whole san marzano tomatoes, drained and chopped
2 tsp. fresh oregano leaves

1. Dissolve yeast in ¼ cup lukewarm water in a large bowl and set aside until foamy, about 10 minutes. Combine all-purpose and cake flours and salt in a bowl. Add 1 cup flour mixture to yeast. Stir with a wooden spoon. Add ½ cup water, then 1 cup flour. Mix well, then work in remaining 1 cup flour. Gradually add another ¼ cup water to make a soft, moist dough.

2. Turn out dough onto a lightly floured surface and knead until smooth, 10–12 minutes. Divide dough into 4 even or equal balls. Lightly coat the inside of 4 small bowls with oil. Place 1 ball of dough in each bowl. Cover with damp cloths and set aside to let rise until dough doubles in bulk, 2½–3 hours.

3. Place pizza stone or unglazed tiles in oven and preheat at highest setting (not broil). On a floured surface, stretch 1 ball of dough into a thin 9" circle. Place 2 slices mozzarella, 4 anchovy filets, and 2–3 tbsp. tomatoes on one side of 1 circle of dough. Sprinkle with oregano, fold dough over, and pinch to seal. Repeat process to make a total of 4 calzone.

4. Sprinkle cornmeal on pizza stone. Brush each calzone with a little oil and place on top of pizza stone. Bake calzone until golden, about 15 minutes.

Beyond the Pizzeria

In a way, pizza is the worst thing that could have happened to Neapolitan cuisine—not because there's anything wrong with pizza itself, heaven knows, but because it has seduced the whole world, obscuring, in the process, the vast, sophisticated, non-pizza culinary repertoire of Naples and the surrounding region. From fried antipasti (salt cod with olives, rice balls, asparagus tips, and more) to baroque timbales of pasta, from complex variations on the meatball to a veritable panoply of eggplant dishes, Neapolitan cooking is one of the great gastronomic riches of Italy—a country in which gastronomic riches are hardly in short supply.

From the Hearth

Focaccia, which is flat, slightly raised bread, not unlike thick pizza crust, is made in many parts of Italy—and has always been especially popular near the sea, where humidity in the air inhibits the full rising of conventional bread dough. The word *focaccia* comes from the Latin *focus*, hearth—probably because it could be baked at home, on flat stones kept hot behind the hearth, and didn't necessarily need the services of a baker's oven. Today, most focaccia is made commercially—but because it cooks quickly, it is usually made several times a day instead of just in the early morning like other breads. Liguria is particularly famous for its focaccia, which is moist with the region's delicate olive oil. The fishing town of Recco, on the Ligurian coast, has a specialty called focaccia col formaggio—which consists of two layers of cracker-thin focaccia enclosing molten white cheese—but most Ligurian focaccia is flavored only with coarse salt or, sometimes, rosemary. Elsewhere in Italy, though, it may have simple toppings of thin-sliced onions, thin-sliced tomatoes (or tomato sauce), black or green olives, even wisps of lemon, peel and all.

Focaccia

SERVES 6

LIGURIA'S neighbor Tuscany gave us hints for this recipe—by way of *Giuliano Bugialli's Food of Tuscany* (Stewart, Tabori & Chang, 1992). One secret for making good focaccia, in whatever region: don't skimp on the olive oil.

1 7-gram packet active dry yeast
¼ cup lukewarm water
4 ½ cups unbleached all-purpose flour
Salt
¾ cup fruity extra-virgin olive oil
3 tbsp. fresh rosemary leaves
1 ¼ cups water
Coarse salt

1. Dissolve yeast in ¼ cup lukewarm water in a large bowl and set aside until foamy, about 10 minutes. Meanwhile, put 2 cups of the flour into a large bowl, making a well in the center. Pour in dissolved yeast mixture, add salt, and stir with a wooden spoon to mix flour gradually into yeast until it forms a wet paste. Sprinkle with 1 tbsp. of the flour, then cover bowl with a cotton kitchen towel and allow "sponge" to rest in a warm place, away from drafts, until it has doubled in size, 1–1½ hours.

2. Heat ¼ cup of the oil in a small saucepan over low heat until warm. Remove from heat, add rosemary leaves, and set aside.

3. When sponge has doubled in size, measure out 2 cups of the flour onto a clean surface. Make a well in the middle of the flour and put sponge in well. Make another well in the sponge and pour in rosemary oil with leaves and 1¼ cups warm water. Using your fingertips, start in the center and mix in circular motion to form a soft, wet dough. Set dough aside. Wipe surface clean, wash and dry your hands, then lightly flour the surface and your hands with remaining flour. Knead dough with the heel of your palm, folding it over onto itself, until it is elastic and smooth, about 2 minutes. Add more flour if dough becomes too sticky.

4. Use ¼ cup of the oil to grease a 15½" x 10½" jelly-roll pan. Roll out the dough with a rolling pin so it fits the pan. Place dough in pan, spreading it out evenly, then use your fingertips to make indentations all over top of focaccia. Drizzle remaining ¼ cup oil over focaccia. Sprinkle with coarse salt. Cover with plastic wrap and the cotton kitchen towel and let rest until doubled in size again, about 1 hour.

5. Preheat oven to 400°. Bake in the middle of the oven until golden, about 30 minutes. Set on a rack to let cool. Drizzle with olive oil and season with more salt, if you like.

Torta Pasqualina
(Eastertide Torte)

SERVES 8

LINDA BELFORTE (right, center and bottom), former chef at Genoa's Yacht Club Italiano—Italy's oldest yacht club—showed us how to make this classic savory pastry.

FOR PASTRY:
6 cups flour
6 tbsp. extra-virgin
  olive oil
2 tsp. salt

FOR FILLING:
Salt
4½ lbs. swiss chard,
  stems removed
½ cup extra-virgin
  olive oil
1 cup freshly grated
  parmigiano-reggiano
¼ cup ricotta
2 tbsp. finely chopped
  fresh oregano
2 tbsp. heavy cream
Freshly ground black
  pepper
5 eggs
2½ tbsp. butter

1. For pastry, put flour into a large bowl, make a well in the center, and add oil, salt, and 2 cups water. Mix thoroughly with a wooden spoon. When dough becomes too stiff to stir, knead on a floured work surface until smooth and soft, about 20 minutes (dough will be quite sticky). Divide into 6 equal balls, wrap in plastic wrap, and refrigerate for at least 2 hours.

2. For filling, bring a large pot of salted water to a boil over high heat. Add chard and cook until tender, 3–4 minutes. Drain and refresh under cold running water. Squeeze out excess water and finely chop.

3. Heat ¼ cup of the oil in a large skillet over medium heat. Add swiss chard and cook, stirring, for 3 minutes. Transfer to a large bowl. Cool swiss chard slightly, then add parmigiano, ricotta, and oregano. Mix thoroughly, stir in cream. Season to taste with salt and pepper. Set aside.

4. Preheat oven to 400°. Lightly grease a 10" pie pan or 12" pizza pan. On a floured surface, roll out a ball of dough as thinly as possible (about 13½" in diameter) and transfer to pan. Brush with a small amount of oil, then repeat with 2 additional balls of dough, layering them on top of the first one.

5. Spread chard mixture on top of rolled dough, leaving a 2" border. Using the back of a spoon, make 5 indentations in the chard mixture. Break an egg into the indentations (**A**) and top each with ½ tbsp. of butter. Season with salt and pepper.

6. Roll out remaining balls of dough as above, lay on top of filling, and brush each one with oil. For an especially light crust, blow into torta (**B**), then quickly seal by twisting outer edge of dough together (**C**). Bake torta until golden, about 45 minutes. Serve in wedges, warm or at room temperature.

VARIATION—Substitute 2 sheets (about 3 lbs.) thawed, frozen puff pastry for dough. Roll out 1 sheet, fill as in step 5, then roll out remaining sheet and place over filling and bake as in step 6.

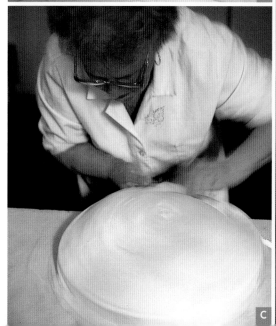

Torta Lore

The notion of savory pies is ancient, perhaps dating to the Mesopotamians. The Egyptians, Greeks, and Romans all ate something similar. More recently, torte (the plural of *torta*) figured prominently in the sophisticated cooking of the courts of Naples and—as tourtes—in the classical kitchens of France. Torte in various designs are made all over Italy today, but the Ligurians seem to produce the thing in its purest form—just dough and filling, unelaborated, undecorated, elemental. The torta pasqualina (see recipe, facing page), the queen of Genoese tarts, was traditionally made with 33 layers of dough—one for each year of Christ's life.

Torta Verde

(Swiss Chard and Potato Torte)

SERVES 8

THE TORTA was poor people's food in the Ligurian backcountry; in fact, it was called *pasta*, in this case meaning "meal"—because a torta was often all there was for dinner.

FOR DOUGH:
1 ¼ cups flour, sifted
½ tsp. salt
1 ½ tbsp. extra-virgin
   olive oil

FOR FILLING:
8–10 large leaves swiss
   chard, stems removed,
   leaves finely chopped
Salt
1 medium russet potato,
   boiled, peeled, and diced
1 medium yellow onion,
   peeled and finely
   chopped
2 tbsp. minced fresh
   Italian parsley
1 ¼ cups crumbled mild
   feta
Freshly ground black
   pepper
2 eggs, lightly beaten
4 tbsp. extra-virgin
   olive oil

1. For dough, mix together flour and salt in a large bowl. Drizzle oil into flour, mixing with a fork, then sprinkle in up to ½ cup water, 1 tbsp. at a time, mixing until dough just holds together. Knead dough until smooth and elastic, about 15 minutes. Shape dough into a ball, cover with a damp cloth, and refrigerate for 2 hours.

2. For filling, put chard into a colander, sprinkle with 1½ tbsp. salt, toss to mix, and set aside to drain for 20 minutes.

3. Meanwhile, mix together potatoes, onions, parsley, and feta in a bowl and season to taste with salt and pepper. Press chard against colander with a wooden spoon to squeeze out juices. Discard juices and add chard to potato mixture. Mix in eggs and 2½ tbsp. oil and set aside.

4. Preheat oven to 375°. Lightly oil and flour a 14" round pizza pan. Divide dough into 2 balls, using two-thirds of dough for bottom crust and one-third for top crust. Roll out dough for bottom crust on a floured surface to about 15" in diameter, then use pizza pan as a template to trim crust to form a 14" round. Place bottom crust in pan. Evenly spread with filling, leaving 1" of crust exposed around edge. Roll out dough for top crust to 13" and place atop filling, allowing it to drape over edge of filling. Wet edge of bottom crust, fold in, and crimp to seal. Using a fork, pierce surface of torta several times to allow steam to escape during cooking. Then use your fingertips to gently indent surface of pie, and drizzle with remaining 1½ tbsp. oil. Bake until golden, about 35 minutes.

The Art of the Torta

On a terraced hillside in the Valle Argentina, on the outskirts of Triora in the *entroterra* of Liguria, Adriana Saldo (facing page, right, with daughter-in-law Erica Oddo) and her sister Anna are bickering good-naturedly over a large, flat, lidded cast-iron pan perched on a tripod over a fire of vine cuttings and twigs. "Every time you poke the fire, that side of the torta burns," scolds one. "No, it's your fault," counters the other. "It's because when you picked up the pan, you didn't put it down again properly." Adriana and Anna are cooking a torta the old-fashioned way, in the garden over an open fire. "The open fire produces a very good torta," says Adriana. "You can smell when it's cooked," adds Anna. After the torta has been on the fire for about 25 minutes, Adriana and Anna agree—more or less— it is done. Later, when we eat it, we find it delicious; the filling is pleasantly sharp but creamy, the crust vaguely smoky—truly savory.

Torta di Patate

(Puréed Potato Torte)

SERVES 8

TORTA DOUGH in the Ligurian mountains has always been rolled out very thin—not only for aesthetic reasons, says Mara Allavena, but also to make the flour go farther.

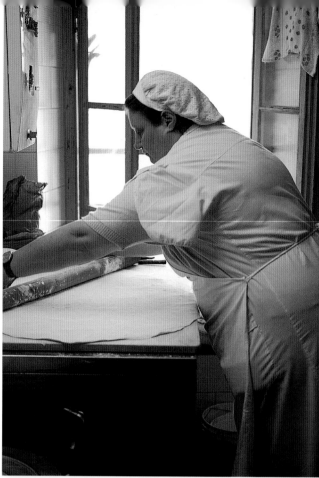

FOR DOUGH:
1 ¼ cups flour, sifted
½ tsp. salt
1 ½ tbsp. extra-virgin
   olive oil

FOR FILLING:
4 medium russet potatoes
Salt
1 egg, lightly beaten
¼ cup freshly grated
   parmigiano-reggiano
¼ cup well-drained
   ricotta
1 cup milk
2 tbsp. butter
Freshly ground black
   pepper
Extra-virgin olive oil

1. For dough, mix together flour and salt in a large bowl. Drizzle oil into flour, mixing with a fork, then sprinkle in up to ½ cup water, 1 tbsp. at a time, mixing until dough just holds together. Knead dough until smooth and elastic, about 15 minutes. Shape dough into a ball, cover with a damp cloth, and refrigerate for 2 hours.

2. For filling, cook potatoes in a large pot of salted water over medium-high heat until soft, about 25 minutes.

3. Preheat oven to 375°. Drain potatoes, allow to cool slightly, then peel. Mash potatoes in a bowl, then mix in egg, parmigiano, ricotta, milk, and butter, stirring until mixture becomes a smooth paste. Season to taste with salt and pepper.

4. Lightly oil and flour a 14" round pizza pan. Roll out dough for crust on a floured surface to about 18" in diameter, then place on pan so that crust hangs evenly over edge of pan all around. Evenly spread filling on crust, leaving 3" of crust exposed around edge. Gently stretch crust over filling and in toward center of pie, gathering it slightly. Continue until filling is almost completely enclosed; leave a small hole in center to allow steam to escape during baking. Being careful not to tear crust, use your fingertips to gently indent surface of pie, then drizzle with 1½ tbsp. oil. Bake until golden, about 35 minutes.

Mountain Magic

I n the mountain village of Castel Vittorio, a glowingly robust restaurateur named Mara Allavena (top left and bottom middle) makes definitive torte at her modest little Osteria del Portico. The osteria is the kind of eatery where men gather at a tiny bar just inside the front door to drink grappa and watch soccer on a pint-size television and where a dozen kids from the local elementary school file in with their teacher every day for lunch. Allavena's torte are famous: instead of having many top and bottom layers, hers are made with a single oversize sheet of dough; the filling is placed in the middle and the edges are drawn up to the center in irregular pleats. She usually bakes her torte in a small oven in her little kitchen, but on special occasions, Allavena would carry them down the street to the local communal oven (see photograph, page 319). This is another reason torte were important in this region, she says: "The baker would cook it for you in the leftover heat after he'd finished his loaves." A delicious economy.

Torta Salata Pasquale

(Easter Bread with Prosciutto and Olives)

SERVES 12

ROMANS traditionally eat sweet bread with salame on Easter morning; Jane Mariani of Antico Ristorante Pagnanelli, in Castel Gondolfo, near Rome, serves this bread instead.

3¾ cups flour
1½ tbsp. baking powder
¾ cup extra-virgin
   olive oil
1¼ cups dry white wine
6 eggs
¼ lb. prosciutto slices,
   sliced into short strips
¼ lb. mortadella slices,
   sliced into short strips
1 cup whole black olives,
   pitted and sliced
   (preferably Italian,
   such as gaeta)
½ cup grated parmigiano-
   reggiano
Freshly ground black
   pepper

1. Preheat oven to 350°. Grease and flour an 8½" × 11" cake pan. Sift flour and baking powder together into a large mixing bowl. Make a well in the center and add olive oil, white wine, and ½ cup water. Stir with a fork until well blended.

2. Beat eggs in another mixing bowl, then stir into flour mixture. Add prosciutto and mortadella to batter along with olives and parmigiano. Season with pepper, pour into pan, and bake until golden, about 1 hour. Cool slightly, then turn out onto a wire rack to let cool completely.

Heading for the Hills

The favored Roman destination for Pasquetta—"Little Easter", which is to say Easter Monday—reports David Downie, has long been the winegrowing Alban Hills, southeast of the capital, dotted with the historic towns of the Castelli Romani. These include Frascati, Grottaferrata, and Castel Gandolfo (site of the papal summer residence since the 17th century). Romans who don't pack their own country picnics often head instead for the trattorias and osterias of the Castelli. One of Downie's favorites is Antico Ristorante Pagnanelli, where owners Aurelio (above, lower right) and Jane Mariani and their four sons, Marco (lower left), Giulio (upper left), Gabriele (upper right), and Matteo, carry on Pasquetta traditions in a paradisaical setting. Locals and Romans alike crowd the rustic-style dining room or the balcony, with its dramatic views of Lake Albano. The restaurant was founded in 1882 by Aurelio's maternal grandparents, and, like them, the Marianis grow much of their own produce and raise their own suckling lambs—and on Pasquetta, they serve all the classic Roman Easter dishes, along with a good selection of white and red wines of the Castelli.

10

DESSERTS

NOBODY knows for sure who invented

ice cream—but we do know that in the

ninth century, the Arabs in Sicily iced their

fruit drinks with the snows of Mt. Etna.

And we know incontrovertibly, too, that

Sicilians adore ice cream to this day. Even at 3 A.M., for instance, Palermo's Gelateria Stancampiano (top left and bottom right) offers 48 flavors, from jasmine to zuppa inglese, served up in slurpy, drippy blobs, in cones or sandwiched in soft brioche buns. —DOROTHY KALINS

RECIPES

Gubana

(Friulian Fruitcake)

SERVES 12

THIS IS OUR adaptation of the traditional panettone-like Friulian cake made by Ennio Furlan at the Agriturismo de Carvalho in Manzano. In Friuli, locals sometimes dip pieces of gubana in grappa before popping it into their mouths.

FOR DOUGH:
1 7-gram packet
   active dry yeast
½ cup sugar
¾ cup milk, warmed
4 egg yolks
4 tbsp. butter, softened
3 ½ cups flour
Grated zest of 1 lemon
Pinch of salt
2 tbsp. dark rum

FOR FILLING:
¾ cup raisins
6 pitted prunes, chopped
6 dried figs, chopped
2 oz. dark rum
¾ cup pine nuts, finely
   chopped
¾ cup walnuts, finely
   chopped
½ cup hazelnuts, finely
   chopped
½ cup almonds, finely
   chopped
3 tbsp. grated semisweet
   chocolate
1 tbsp. candied fruits
¼ cup crushed amaretti
   cookies
¼ cup sugar
4 tbsp. butter, melted
1 tsp. vanilla extract
Pinch of salt
2 eggs, lightly beaten

1. For dough, dissolve yeast with 1 tbsp. of the sugar in ¼ cup of the warm milk. Combine egg yolks, butter, and remaining sugar in the bowl of a standing mixer and beat on medium until well mixed. Continuing to beat, gradually add 3 cups of the flour, then add lemon zest, salt, rum, and dissolved yeast. Gradually mix in remaining ½ cup milk until dough is smooth.

2. Turn dough out onto a lightly floured surface and knead for 5–7 minutes. Transfer dough to a large bowl, cover with a kitchen towel, and set in a warm place until doubled in size, 1–2 hours.

3. For filling, combine raisins, prunes, figs, and rum in a large bowl and set aside to macerate for 1 hour, then mix in pine nuts, walnuts, hazelnuts, almonds, chocolate, candied fruits, amaretti, 3 tbsp. of the sugar, butter, vanilla, and salt.

4. Preheat oven to 375°. Roll out risen dough on a lightly floured surface into a 12" x 16" rectangle. Brush around edges with beaten egg, then spread filling evenly over dough, avoiding edges. Working from long side, roll up dough jelly-roll style, then curl into a spiral. Place on a baking sheet, cover with a kitchen towel, and set aside to let rise for 30 minutes.

5. Brush with beaten egg, sprinkle with remaining 1 tbsp. sugar, and bake until browned, about 50 minutes.

Eating in Friuli

Nestled up against the Carnic Alps, bordering Austria and Slovenia up in far northeastern Italy, the region officially known as Friuli–Venezia Giulia produces some of Italy's best white wines (and a handful of memorable reds) and some of its heartiest cooking. Polenta is far more common than pasta in the traditional local diet, and beans and potatoes are more basic to the cuisine than green vegetables. Cheese and meat are important, as is wild game, and sausages are often accompanied by brovada, a uniquely Friulian creation of turnips fermented in wine must—an initially daunting idea, with echoes of both sauerkraut and kimchi—that can grow pleasantly addictive.

Holiday Tradition

Genoa's quintessential pastry-shop specialty—particularly popular between Christmas and Twelfth Night—is pandolce, a traditional sweet bread originally designed as a showpiece for exotic imported fruits, nuts, and spices. In its original version, it's drier, denser, and a little more crumbly than panettone, its brioche-like Milanese cousin. Like panettone, though, it is usually store-bought rather than homemade—and often packaged in beautiful, ribbon-tied boxes. Pandolce is as much a part of Italian holiday celebrations as fruitcake is in America.

Antico Pandolce Genovese

(Old-Fashioned Genoese Sweet Bread)

SERVES 8

ALTHOUGH LIGHT, airy adaptations of this Christmas sweet are now in vogue throughout Italy, this recipe, from Marco and Maurizio Profumo's Pasticceria Villa di Profumo, a popular pastry shop on Genoa's famed via Garibaldi, produces a more traditional, dense and crumbly version.

½ tsp. active dry yeast
½ cup warm milk
8 tbsp. butter, softened,
  plus additional
  for greasing pan
¾ cup sugar
1 tbsp. fennel seeds
½ tsp. ground coriander
1 egg, lightly beaten
2 tsp. vanilla extract
4 tsp. orange flower water
3½ cups flour
½ cup dried currants
⅓ cup golden raisins
⅓ cup finely chopped
  candied orange rind
⅓ cup pine nuts

1. Dissolve yeast in milk in a small bowl. Set aside until foamy, about 10 minutes.

2. Meanwhile, beat butter in an electric mixer and gradually add sugar, beating until mixture is light and fluffy. Add fennel seeds and coriander, then add egg, vanilla, and orange flower water and mix thoroughly. Add milk and dissolved yeast and mix. (Mixture may appear slightly curdled.)

3. Gradually add flour, mixing thoroughly. When dough is smooth, mix in currants, raisins, orange rind, and pine nuts (dough will be moist). Transfer dough to a large greased bowl. Cover with a clean kitchen towel and set aside in a warm place to let rise for 3–4 hours. (Dough may rise only a little.)

4. Preheat oven to 375°. Moisten hands (dough will be sticky) and transfer to a greased cookie sheet. Shape into a 6" round and bake until golden, 45 minutes to 1 hour. Cool completely. To serve, cut or break into small pieces and serve with sweet wine, if desired. (Store in an airtight container.)

Vistorta Torta di Cioccolato

(Flourless Chocolate Cake)

SERVES 6–8

WHEN THEY invited us to lunch at their palazzo in Venice, the Count and Countess Brandolini (right, in their Venetian garden) served us this dense confection—named for their wine estate in Friuli and based on an old family recipe.

13 tbsp. butter, softened
3 tbsp. flour
6 oz. semisweet chocolate
¾ cup sugar
6 eggs, separated
1 ¼ cups finely ground almonds
1 tbsp. brandy
2 pinches salt
Confectioners' sugar

1. Preheat oven to 375°. Using about 1 tbsp. of the butter, butter an 11" springform pan, line bottom with parchment paper, butter paper, then dust paper and sides of pan with flour. Melt chocolate in top of double boiler set above simmering water over medium heat. Set aside to let cool.

2. Put remaining 12 tbsp. butter into a large bowl and beat with an electric mixer until fluffy. Gradually add sugar, beating for 2–3 minutes. Add egg yolks one at a time, beating well between each addition, then add chocolate, beating just enough to blend it in. Stir in almonds and brandy, then set aside.

3. Put egg whites and salt into a large, clean bowl and beat with an electric mixer until they form medium-stiff peaks. Add a third of the whites to the chocolate mixture and fold in with a rubber spatula, then carefully fold in remaining whites in 2 batches, taking care not to deflate the batter. Pour into prepared pan.

4. Put pan into oven and bake for 15 minutes, reduce heat to 350°, and continue baking until a skewer stuck into center of cake comes out clean, 30–40 minutes. Remove cake from oven and set aside to let cool. Unmold, peel off parchment, and place, right side up, on a cake plate. Dust liberally with confectioners' sugar just before serving.

Wine and Glass

The Brandolini family, whose ancestors were masters of arms (*brando* means "sword" in Italian) near Ravenna, on the Adriatic coast of Emilia-Romagna, bought the 15th-century Palazzo Giustinian (see page 140) in 1850. Today, Brandino, the present-day Count Brandolini, and his wife, Marie Angliviel de la Beaumelle, divide their time between the palazzo—an ornate Gothic palace on the portion of the Grand Canal known as La Volta (The Bend)—and the Brandolini country estate at Vistorta, in Friuli. Brandino, who studied agricultural economics at Texas A&M, supervises the production of the excellent, full-flavored Vistorta merlot, while Marie has become one of the most talented contemporary-glass designers in Venice, selling her work under the name Laguna B. When the two entertain, at either home, the cooking is likely to be a mix of the traditional and the invented, and very good.

Fresh Fruit Tarts

Almost any berry or fruit will make a good fresh fruit crostata. The first ingredient you'll need is just-ripened fruit in season—from strawberries in the summer to figs (below) in the fall. The second is crema pasticceria, or pastry cream. To make it, bring 3 cups of milk to a simmer in a medium pot set over a pot of simmering water over medium heat (this will take about 20 minutes). Combine ⅓ cup of sugar and ¼ cup of flour in a medium bowl. Whisk together 1 egg and 2 egg yolks in a small bowl. Add eggs to sugar–flour mixture and whisk until smooth. Slowly pour 1 cup of the hot milk into the flour-egg mixture, whisking constantly; then gradually add mixture back into the hot milk over simmering water. Cook, whisking constantly, until custard has thickened and no longer tastes of flour, 2–3 minutes. Transfer custard to a mixing bowl and stir in ¼ tsp. vanilla extract. Cover surface of cream with plastic wrap to prevent a skin from forming and refrigerate until cool. To assemble a fresh fruit tart, follow step 1 of the recipe at right, then put tart pan directly onto the pizza stone in the oven and bake for 25 minutes. Remove from oven and let cool on a rack. Slather the dough with crema pasticceria, then top with thinly sliced raw fresh fruit or whole berries.

Crostata con Marmellata di Lamponi

(Raspberry Jam Tart)

MAKES 1 OR 2 TARTS

JAM TARTS are the quintessential home-baked Italian pastry, served both as dessert and breakfast sweet. Jim Lahey, co-owner of New York City's Italian-flavored Sullivan Street Bakery, learned this recipe from Bruna Bonì, a home cook in the Tuscan town of San Casciano dei Bagni.

1 recipe pasta frolla
  (see page 300, steps
  1 and 2)
½–1 cup raspberry jam

1. Place a pizza stone in oven and preheat to 350°. Cut dough in half and form 2 balls (either make 2 tarts or wrap and freeze one of the balls of dough to use at another time). Roll out 1 ball of dough to ¼" thick round on a lightly floured surface. Lay the bottom of a 9" or 10" false-bottomed tart pan on top of dough. Use a small knife to cut around the edge, saving the scraps. Fold round of dough over rolling pin and carefully transfer dough round into tart pan.

2. Spread ½ cup of jam over center of dough, leaving a 2" border around edge. Roll dough scraps into a ball, then roll out again on a lightly floured surface. Cut dough into thin strips and arrange on top of jam in a lattice pattern.

3. Put tart pan directly onto hot pizza stone in the oven and bake for 25 minutes. Remove from oven and let cool on a rack, to allow the soft crust to harden. Once cooled completely, the crostata will keep for a day or two in a dry airtight container and can be recrisped in a warm oven by being heating through and allowed to cool again.

Ossi di Morti

(Almond Meringue Cookies)

MAKES ABOUT 20

THESE BRITTLE treats owe their morbid-sounding name, which means "bones of the dead", to the fact that they're made every year to celebrate All Souls' Day, November 2, in remembrance of the deceased. Some versions are actually formed into the shape of shank bones—or whole skeletons.

¾ cup sugar
⅓ cup flour
¾ tsp. baking powder
2 egg whites
1 ¼ cups whole almonds

1. Preheat oven to 325°. Sift together sugar, flour, and baking powder into a large mixing bowl. Add the egg whites and beat with a wooden spoon until thoroughly combined, then stir in almonds. Cookie dough will be quite loose.

2. Spoon dough by the tablespoonful onto parchment-lined baking sheets, 2"–3" apart. Bake until light golden brown, 16–18 minutes.

3. Remove cookies from oven and set aside on racks to let cool completely before peeling off parchment.

Italy's Cookie Jar

I talians may not have a big sweet tooth in general, but they do love their cookies, or biscotti (the word is applied to cookies in general in Italy, not just to the long, flat treats we call by that name; see page 294). Some Italians even consider cookies dunked in caffè latte to be breakfast. Here are some of their favorites:

◆ AMARETTI: These light, round almond cookies got their name, which means "little bitter ones", from their key ingredient, bitter almonds. The most famous amaretti come from the town of Saronno in Lombardy, where they are said to have been invented in the 1700s. Really small ones are called amarettini.

◆ BRUTTI MA BUONI: These "ugly but good" vanilla-scented almond or hazelnut meringue cookies, named for their irregular shape, are Piedmontese in origin.

◆ CANTUCCINI: A specialty of the town of Prato, near Florence, these "little scraps" are small, dry, hard almond-studded biscotti and are often dipped in vin santo to soften them.

◆ RICCIARELLI: These diamond-shaped marzipan cookies from Siena date back to the Renaissance and are perhaps Arab in origin. Their name, which derives from *riccio*, or curly, suggests they might originally have had a different shape.

◆ SAVOIARDI: These long, light cookies, used to make tiramisù (see page 296), earned their name and fame in the 14th century, when the House of Savoy ruled Piedmont. In America we call them ladyfingers.

Anise-Almond Biscotti

MAKES ABOUT 2 DOZEN

WHEN Pittsburgh baker Larry Lagattuta (far right, center) decided, back in 1993, that his destiny was to make biscotti, he happily discovered this recipe—which his grandmother used decades ago back in Reggio Calabria. The recipe shows why these cookies are called *biscotti*, or twice baked.

¾ cup whole almonds
2 ¼ cups flour
1 ½ tsp. baking powder
¼ tsp. salt
8 tbsp. butter, softened
¼ cup sugar
2 eggs, lightly beaten
1 tsp. vanilla extract
1 tbsp. anise seeds

1. Preheat oven to 350°. Spread almonds in a single layer on a baking sheet and toast, turning occasionally, for 10 minutes. Set aside to let cool, then roughly chop.

2. Sift together flour, baking powder, and salt in a small mixing bowl. Set aside. Cream butter and sugar together in a large mixing bowl with an electric mixer until fluffy, then beat in eggs and vanilla. Gradually add flour mixture, mix until combined, then stir in chopped almonds and anise seeds. (Dough will be stiff.)

3. Transfer dough to a lightly floured surface, then, using your hands or a rolling pin, shape into 1 long roll, about 3" × 13".

4. Line baking sheet with parchment paper or aluminum foil (shiny side up). Transfer dough roll to baking sheet, flatten slightly, then bake until golden brown, about 35 minutes. Remove from oven—do not turn oven off—and set aside until cool enough to handle, about 15 minutes.

5. Using a serrated knife, cut roll, on the diagonal, into ½"-thick slices. Place slices flat on baking sheet and bake, turning once, until golden brown, about 5 minutes per side. Do not overbake: biscotti will feel soft in the middle but will become crisp and hard as they cool. Allow to cool completely on baking sheet. Biscotti will keep in a sealed container for up to 4 weeks.

The Strip

I t's early Saturday morning, and crowds are swirling around outside the Italian, Mexican, and Asian markets and food shops of Pittsburgh's Strip district, a ten-block area along the Allegheny River on the edge of downtown. Funky, busy, and full of good things to eat, reports Pittsburgh writer Marlene Parrish, these places are community institutions; some are in their fourth generation of family ownership. Outside one shop, the sweet smell of chocolate drifts into the crowd. Above the door, a hand-lettered sign depicting a huge, winged cookie announces the presence inside of the Enrico Biscotti Company— but in the kitchen, it is not an Enrico but a 42-year-old Italian-American named Larry Lagattuta who has been baking, and rebaking, biscotti for the past three hours. Each week, Lagattuta produces more than 7,000 pounds of biscotti, which come in some 32 varieties—from the anise-flavored classic at left to designer creations with white chocolate and macadamia nuts. They're as good as any we've ever had in Italy.

Cream, Not Cheese

Mascarpone is sometimes described as cheese, but it's actually the solids that remain when liquid is removed from heavy cream. Believed to have originated in Lombardy, in the mountainous region between Lodi and Abbiategrasso, it may take its name from the local dialect word for ricotta, *mascherpa*, since it resembles that cheese (see sidebar, page 299) in texture. Mascarpone is used commonly in desserts—most notably in the ubiquitous tiramisù—but it is also sometimes layered with gorgonzola, prosciutto, or other substances as an antipasto; and the Milanese have been known to stir it into pasta and other savory dishes in place of butter.

Tiramisù

SERVES 4

APPARENTLY invented in Treviso (right), at El Toulà— a hotel restaurant noted for its good cooking—this dessert, whose name means "pick me up" (perhaps a reference to its caffeine content), has become so famous in America that it seems to appear on almost every menu. This simple, classic version of tiramisù comes from Alle Testiere in Venice.

2 eggs, separated
½ cup sugar
½ cup mascarpone
1 cup strong, fresh black coffee (not espresso)
12 Italian savoiardi cookies or ladyfingers
Cocoa powder

1. Beat egg yolks with a whisk in a medium bowl. Gradually add sugar, continuing to whisk until mixture is thick, smooth, and pale yellow. Gently fold mascarpone into mixture with a rubber spatula, then set aside.

2. Put egg whites into a clean, dry mixing bowl and beat with a whisk until they form stiff but not dry peaks. Fold egg whites into mascarpone mixture and set aside.

3. Pour coffee into a wide, shallow bowl. Dip 4 of the savoiardi into the coffee just long enough to moisten them without making them soggy, then arrange them side by side in a single layer on a serving platter. Spread one-third of the mascarpone mixture over the biscuits, then dust with a little cocoa powder. Repeat the entire process twice, dipping the savoiardi in coffee and layering them with mascarpone and cocoa. Refrigerate until well chilled.

Frittelle di Ricotta

(Ricotta Fritters)

MAKES ABOUT 36 2" FRITTERS

THESE SURPRISINGLY light fritters are best constructed with freshly made ricotta; if only commercial ricotta is available, drain off any excess moisture before proceeding.

3 eggs, lightly beaten
2 tbsp. sugar
1 lb. ricotta
1 cup flour
4 tbsp. baking powder
5 tbsp. brandy
2 tsp. finely chopped
    lemon zest
Salt
Vegetable oil
Confectioners' sugar

1. Combine eggs, sugar, ricotta, flour, baking powder, brandy, lemon zest, and a pinch of salt in a medium bowl. Mix well, cover, and refrigerate for 1 hour.

2. Pour oil into a large saucepan to a depth of 3". Heat oil over medium-high heat until hot but not smoking, about 375° on a candy thermometer. Drop rounded teaspoonfuls of batter into hot oil and fry, a few at a time, until golden, about 5 minutes.

3. Drain on paper towels, dust with confectioners' sugar, and serve.

The Right Whey

Ricotta is basically an ingenious use of leftovers—specifically of whey, the thin, greenish liquid that remains when milk coagulates into the curds that become cheese. The whey, when reheated with a bit of sour whey to help it coagulate, often with some whole milk added, yields soft, tiny clusters of ricotta (literally, "re-cooked") cheese, with an ethereal delicacy and a faint, irresistible sweetness. In Emilia-Romagna, where it is used frequently in pasta fillings, ricotta is often made from cows'-milk parmigiano-reggiano whey. In Sicily, where sheep's-milk ricotta is preferred (the cheese can also be made from the milk of goats or water buffalo), it's a main ingredient in desserts like cannoli and cassata (see page 300). Besides fresh ricotta, Italians make ricotta salata, aged salted ricotta that is usually grated over pasta; ricotta forte, pungent fermented ricotta, often mixed with herbs, for smearing on bread; and ricotta affumicata, smoked ricotta. High-temperature pasteurization, to which commercial ricotta in the United States is invariably subjected, kills the flavor of this tender cheese, so it's worth seeking out slow-pasteurized ricotta from specialty food stores or Italian markets. Some recipes in this country, incidentally, suggest that you substitute cottage cheese for ricotta. Don't. As Marcella Hazan once declared, "This is a most grievous error. Cottage cheese is completely un-Italian in taste and should not be contemplated as a replacement for ricotta."

Recipes as Legacy

Say 'frittata'," Giovanna Tornabene (above, right) and her mother, Wanda, squeal in unison as our photographer makes the portrait that will be on the cover of their second American cookbook, *Sicilian Home Cooking* (Alfred A. Knopf, 2001), in their kitchen in Gangivecchio, in the onetime Benedictine abbey built in the 14th century that, since 1856, has been home to four generations of Tornabenes. "It has always been my intention to pass my recipe collection on to my children ... one day," says Wanda. In fact, until the Tornabenes published their first cookbook, in 1996, no one outside the family had ever benefited from the worn notebook full of handwritten recipes and family anecdotes. In the terracotta splendor of Benedictine architecture, the Tornabenes, including Wanda's son, Paolo, run a small inn and a restaurant (busiest on Sundays, luring people from Palermo who long for the mountains). Surrounded by elegant relics and photographs of another time, Wanda refuses to cook in the restaurant's newer kitchen, turning out her Sicilian specialties, like the classic cassata al forno at right (as well as things like arancine, page 55, and involtini alla benedettina, page 219), from a workaday room, with well-worn pans—her favorite kitchen utensil being her own hands.

Cassata al Forno
(Baked Ricotta Cake)

SERVES 6

OF THE three Sicilian cassatas, two, cassata gelata and cassata alla siciliana, are better bought in pastry shops. This simple, sweetened ricotta cheese cake is the one to make at home.

FOR PASTA FROLLA:
1 ½ cups flour
⅔ cups sugar
2 tsp. baking powder
2 eggs
1 tsp. grated lemon zest
3 drops vanilla extract
6 tbsp. butter, melted

FOR CREMA DI RICOTTA:
2 cups whole-milk ricotta
½ cup sugar
½ tsp. vanilla extract
¼ cup chocolate chips
¼ cup diced candied citron

Confectioners' sugar

1. For pasta frolla, sift flour, sugar, and baking powder into a large mixing bowl, then make a well in the center. Lightly whisk together eggs, lemon zest, and vanilla in a separate bowl. Pour eggs into center of well in flour mixture. Gradually incorporate eggs into flour, using 2 knives, until mixture is dry and crumbly. Gradually add melted butter until a soft, wet dough is formed.

2. Turn out dough onto a lightly floured surface, lightly flour your hands, and knead just enough to form a smooth dough. Use a pastry scraper to help lift and knead dough, adding a little more flour if dough sticks to floured surface. (The dough will be very soft.) Wrap in plastic and refrigerate overnight.

3. For crema di ricotta, put ricotta in a strainer lined with cheesecloth, set over a bowl. Cover with plastic wrap and refrigerate overnight to allow excess water to drain off.

4. Remove ricotta from refrigerator, pour off water, then transfer ricotta to bowl. Add sugar, vanilla, chocolate chips, and citron to ricotta and mix well.

5. Preheat oven to 350°. Butter and flour a 9" springform cake pan, then set aside. Roll out three-quarters of the dough on a lightly floured surface into a round about 12" in diameter and ¼" thick. Gently fold dough over rolling pin, then fit it into bottom of cake pan, with 2"–3" of the dough coming up the side of the pan. Spoon in filling, spreading it evenly over dough. Fold pastry edges in over edge of ricotta filling. Roll out remaining dough to a thickness of about ¼". Cut into ½"-wide strips. Decorate top of cake with strips in a lattice pattern. Bake on a baking sheet in the middle of the oven until golden, 45–55 minutes. Remove from oven and let cool on a cake rack for 10 minutes. Sprinkle with confectioners' sugar before serving.

Granita

(Italian Ice)

SERVES 6

THE MOST important thing to remember about making Italian ices is that their flavor must be as intense as possible. Lemon granita should be slightly on the sour side; coffee granita should taste as enticing as good espresso smells.

FOR LEMON GRANITA:
1 ½ cups fresh lemon juice
   (juice of 8–9 lemons)
½ cup sugar

FOR COFFEE GRANITA:
4 cups (32 oz.) freshly
   brewed espresso, at room
   temperature
1 cup sugar

1. For lemon granita, put lemon juice, sugar, and 1 cup water into a medium bowl and stir with a wooden spoon until sugar dissolves, about 3 minutes.

2. Pour into a medium-deep dish and transfer to the freezer. Using the tines of a fork, stir mixture every 30 minutes, scraping edges and breaking up any chunks as mixture freezes, until granita is slushy and frozen, about 4 hours.

3. For coffee granita, put espresso and sugar into a medium bowl and stir with a wooden spoon until sugar dissolves, about 3 minutes, then proceed as in step 2.

4. Divide granitas into individual serving glasses or transfer into a plastic container, cover, and freeze until ready to serve.

Sicilian Ice

Deep in the medieval quarter of Palermo, around the corner from the twisted streets that loosely make up the earthy market known as La Vucciria, lies the beautiful piazza San Francesco—defined on one side by the church of that name and on another by the Antica Focacceria San Francesco (facing page). In its 19th-century interior, the Focacceria serves such succulent local lunch specialties as arancine (see page 55), the chickpea-flour fritters called panelle, and sfincionelli, squares of focaccia topped with anchovies, baby artichokes, onions, and tomato sauce. Just across the square is dessert—from the Focacceria's ice cream and pastry shop, the Gelateria San Francesco, which dishes up heavenly examples of the vaunted flavored ice called granita, which some say was invented not far from here. A variety of flavors is offered, but lemon and coffee, above, served with the typical soft bun, are the most popular in Sicily.

Inventing Ices

The American writer Mary Taylor Simeti, author of a superlative history of Sicilian food called *Pomp and Sustenance* (Ecco Press, 1989), explains that the Sicilians have always taken their ice cream very seriously. When the Piedmontese King Vittorio Amedeo inherited the Sicilian crown for a brief period at the beginning of the 18th century, he described the lackadaisical Sicilian legislators as an "ice cream and sorbet parliament", but these were men who knew their priorities. When in the fall of 1774 Palermo's supply of snow for sweet ices gave out, the parliament dispatched an armed party of dragoons to Catania to procure some more. The demand was high: it is said that for just one ball, given in 1799 in honor of the Bourbon King Ferdinand and his wife Maria Carolina, 5000 pounds of snow were consumed.

Gelato

(Italian-Style Ice Cream)

SERVES 8–12

WE SAMPLED an embarrassing number of gelati at Gelateria Stancampiano (left and right) in the heart of Palermo, at the insistence of Giovanni Stancampiano himself, before settling on pistachio and chocolate as our favorites.

FOR PISTACHIO
GELATO:
4 cups milk
1 cup sugar
3 tbsp. cornstarch
*2 cups shelled, unsalted
    pistachios, finely ground*

FOR CHOCOLATE
GELATO:
3 cups milk
¾ cup sugar
2 tbsp. cornstarch
*¾ cup unsweetened cocoa
    powder*

1. For pistachio gelato, heat 3 cups of the milk in a medium, heavy-bottomed saucepan over medium heat until bubbles appear around the edge of the pan and milk is just about to boil. Meanwhile, put remaining cup of milk, the sugar, and cornstarch into a small bowl, stir until well combined, then set aside. When milk is ready, remove from heat and stir in cornstarch mixture. Return pan to heat and cook, stirring frequently, until sugar dissolves and mixture thickens slightly, 8–10 minutes.

2. Put pistachios into a large bowl and stir in the hot-milk mixture. Set aside to let cool, stirring often, then cover with plastic wrap, and refrigerate overnight.

3. Strain pistachio-milk mixture through a fine sieve into a medium bowl, pressing pistachios with the back of a wooden spoon to extract as much of the flavor as possible. Discard ground nuts. Pour strained pistachio-milk mixture into an ice cream maker and process according to manufacturer's directions.

4. For chocolate gelato, follow step 1, using 2 cups of the milk, combining remaining cup of milk with sugar, cornstarch, and cocoa powder, and cooking mixture until sugar and cocoa dissolves. Set aside to let cool, then cover with plastic wrap and refrigerate overnight. Pour mixture into an ice cream maker and process according to manufacturer's instructions.

Gelato di Crema al Tartufo Bianco

(Cream Gelato with White Truffles)

SERVES 4

WE WERE skeptical when Manhattan's stylish San Pietro restaurant offered us white truffle ice cream for dessert one night—but one bite sold us. If you're not convinced, or if white truffles are out of season (or out of your price range), try this gelato anyway: it's almost as good without the tubers.

4 cups heavy cream
4 egg yolks
5 tbsp. sugar
1 oz. fresh white truffles
1 tsp. vanilla extract
1 tsp. high-quality
   truffle oil

1. Bring cream to a simmer in a medium heavy saucepan over medium heat. Meanwhile, put egg yolks and sugar into a medium mixing bowl and whisk until thick, smooth, and pale yellow, about 5 minutes.

2. Slowly pour 1 cup of the hot cream into the yolk mixture, whisking constantly; then gradually add mixture back into the hot cream in the saucepan, stirring with a wooden spoon. Reduce heat to low and cook, stirring constantly, until custard is thick enough to coat the back of the spoon, about 10 minutes. Do not allow custard to boil (it will curdle).

3. Strain custard through a sieve into a medium bowl. Set aside to let cool, then cover and refrigerate for at least 4 hours. Clean truffle with a soft mushroom brush (do not wash in water), rid the crevices of any remaining pockets of dirt with the tip of a paring knife, and brush again. Shave truffle and set aside a little more than half of it. Add vanilla to cold custard, then pour into an ice cream maker and process according to manufacturer's directions, adding truffle oil and shavings a few minutes before churning is completed. Serve gelato with a few shavings of remaining truffle over the top, if you like.

Truffle Power

O n the day after Christmas in 1976, Gerardo Bruno (below) left his native Salerno, on Italy's famed Amalfi Coast, where he and his three brothers had learned to cook in his mother's kitchen and he had then gone on to train in local restaurants. He ended up in Manhattan, cooking and learning the American restaurant trade, and opened Sistina in 1984 and San Pietro in 1992. Both have been successful; San Pietro in particular has become a prime "power lunch" spot and celebrity hangout. Bruno makes an effort to offer his customers unusual dishes, many from his native region. As for gelato with truffles, Bruno says the dessert is nothing new in Italy—but adds that he will serve it for only a brief period each year. "Truffle season starts on October 15," says Bruno, "but I like to wait until the middle of the season, when the truffles are mature and more flavorful."

Thanks to the English

Like sherry, port, and madeira, marsala—which is a sweet, fortified wine made around the town of the same name on Sicily's northwestern coast—may be said to be an English invention. It was the English, that is, who discovered that by fortifying grape wine—in Italy, as in Spain and Portugal—with brandy or other spirits, they had created a product that would survive the long ocean voyage to the English marketplace without spoiling. The specific credit in the case of marsala is given to wine merchant John Woodhouse, cofounder of the celebrated shipping firm Smith Woodhouse, who first shipped fortified marsala to the English in 1773. It never achieved the popularity in northern climes that its Iberian counterparts did, but in Italy, marsala has long been the quality cooking wine of choice for dishes both savory and sweet—for veal scaloppine, for instance, as well as for zabaione and various pastries.

Zabaione
(Marsala Custard)

SERVES 4

THE NAME *zabaione*, sometimes also spelled *zabaglione*, possibly derives from *sbaglione*, meaning "big mistake"—something to do with the way it was discovered, no doubt. It is popular all over Italy but may have been invented in Florence, despite its use of marsala, which comes from Sicily.

4 egg yolks
¼ cup sugar
½ cup marsala

1. Put eggs and sugar into a large stainless-steel mixing bowl and, using a large whisk, beat until thick and pale yellow, about 5 minutes.

2. Bring a large pot of water just to a simmer over medium heat (do not let it boil). Set bowl with eggs and sugar over the simmering water to make a double boiler. Gradually drizzle in the marsala, whisking continuously. Continue whisking until the mixture is light and foamy, almost tripling in volume and holding soft peaks, about 15 minutes. (Do not let egg cook around the edges of the bowl.) Spoon into 4 bowls and serve either warm, at room temperature, or chilled.

Photography Credits

PERMISSIONS AND ACKNOWLEDGMENTS:

We drew on the following books in the production of this cookbook: *The Art of Eating Well* by Pellegrino Artusi, published by Random House, 1996; *Lidia's Italian Table* by Lidia Bastianich, published by William Morrow and Company, 1998; *Giuliano Bugialli's Classic Techniques of Italian Cooking* by Giuliano Bugialli, published by Simon & Schuster, 1982; *Giuliano Bugialli's Food of Tuscany* by Giuliano Bugialli, published by Stewart, Tabori & Chang, 1992; *The Classic Italian Cookbook: The Art of Italian Cooking and the Italian Art of Eating* by Marcella Hazan, published by Harper & Row Publishers, Inc., 1973; *Marcella Cucina* by Marcella Hazan, published by HarperCollins, 1997; *The Dictionary of Italian Food and Drink* by John Mariani, published by Broadway Books, 1998; *Grande enciclopedia illustrata della gastronomia*, published by Selezione dal Reader's Digest S.p.A., 1990; *On Persephone's Island* by Mary Taylor Simeti, published by Vintage Departures, 1995; *Pomp and Sustenance: Twenty-Five Centuries of Sicilian Food* by Mary Taylor Simeti, published by The Ecco Press, 1989; *La Cucina Siciliana di Gangivecchio* by Wanda and Giovanna Tornabene with Michele Evans, published by Alfred A. Knopf, 1996; *Sicilian Home Cooking* by Wanda and Giovanna Tornabene with Michele Evans, published by Alfred A. Knopf, 2001. We would also like to acknowledge the forthcoming publication of *Cucina Romana* by David Downie, to be published by HarperCollins, fall 2002.

Index

Table of Equivalents

THE EXACT EQUIVALENTS IN THE FOLLOWING TABLES HAVE BEEN ROUNDED FOR CONVENIENCE.

LIQUID AND DRY MEASURES

U.S.	METRIC
¼ teaspoon	1.25 milliliters
½ teaspoon	2.5 milliliters
1 teaspoon	5 milliliters
1 tablespoon (3 teaspoons)	15 milliliters
1 fluid ounce (2 tablespoons)	30 milliliters
¼ cup	65 milliliters
⅓ cup	80 milliliters
1 cup	235 milliliters
1 pint (2 cups)	480 milliliters
1 quart (4 cups, 32 ounces)	950 milliliters
1 gallon (4 quarts)	3.8 liters
1 ounce (by weight)	28 grams
1 pound	454 grams
2.2 pounds	1 kilogram

LENGTH MEASURES

U.S.	METRIC
⅛ inch	3 millimeters
¼ inch	6 millimeters
½ inch	12 millimeters
1 inch	2.5 centimeters

OVEN TEMPERATURES

FAHRENHEIT	CELSIUS	GAS
250	120	½
275	140	1
300	150	2
325	160	3
350	180	4
375	190	5
400	200	6
425	220	7
450	230	8
475	240	9
500	260	10